THE WADE ROADS

Joan and Arthur Baker

THE MELVEN PRESS

PERTH 1982

Typesetting by David Watt & Sons Ltd., Dunfermline.

Printed by John G. Eccles, Inverness.

Designed by Jenny Carter, Edinburgh.

Published by
THE MELVEN PRESS
176 High Street, Perth, Scotland.

ISBN 0906664187

Contents

Acknowledgements

The publisher would like to thank James Douglas, of Glenfarg, for his careful preparation of the maps which accompany each chapter.

The photographs were prepared by Arthur Baker from his collection with some additional prints provided by Barry Knight and Nick Nicholas.

The publisher would also like to thank Jenny Carter, of Edinburgh, for her invaluable editorial advice.

Introduction

This book originated during the first of our numerous visits to the Central Highlands. It was while consulting the Ordnance Survey map for footpaths and minor roads that we were reminded of 'General Wade's Military Roads'. It is a walkers' book and has been written partly for the pleasure of re-living the experiences from which it grew, partly to answer the many questions about Wade that we asked ourselves and also from a belief that there are many visitors to Scotland who want to do more than tour all day in a car, yet do not know where to start. We suggest one possibility—walking the Wade Roads. There is a growing interest in them and they are in process of being made a Scheduled Monument.

In the sections on each of the roads we have attempted to be practical, and to err on the side of giving too much rather than too little in the way of directions. At the same time we have tried to avoid seeing the roads simply as pathways across the hills. They are part of the history of Scotland, part of the history of Britain, part of a long and often bloody process by which Scotland and England learnt to come to terms with each other. In the preceding pages we have provided some information—the merest 'tip of the iceberg'—on Wade and his time. Here we have sought to provide something that will stimulate the imagination and increase understanding as you walk.

The walks vary from a mile or less along dry, level tracks, through several miles over longish heather with wet stretches, to the twelve rough miles over the Corrieyairack Pass with over 2000 feet of climbing: only the latter makes more than modest demands on physical stamina.

———————— Wade road in
original state.

——————— Wade road under
modern road.

- - - - - - - - Probable line of Wade
road. No evidence visible.

 Wade bridge intact or at
least passable on foot.

> ## Key to symbols on Wade road diagrammatic maps.

 Broken bridge or remnant only
River or burn easily crossed.

 Broken bridge. Crossing
difficult or impossible.

Road running through urban area.

The roads before Wade

It has been said with truth that the history of road-making in the Highlands starts with General Wade.[1] There would, of course, have been some tracks or pathways leading from the villages to the trysts and to the coast before the eighteenth century. But compared even with the Lowlands, and certainly with England, the Highlands were lacking in any real means of communication. The benefits of road-building conferred upon England by the Romans never reached the north of Scotland; but their practice of building roads straight was ultimately, through Wade, to influence road-making in the Highlands also. His roads were built as military roads, although they were used by civilians. If the needs of the civilians had been considered, the roads would not have been built until many years later.

Prior to Wade, the Justices of the Peace had, in theory, the responsibility for making and maintaining the local roads. Their powers of enforcement were very limited, and in the Highlands particularly very little, if any, work was actually done. The Highlanders were, at best, apathetic, the terrain was difficult and travel on foot or on horseback sufficed them. Johnson's account of travel in the unroaded country north-west of the Great Glen, though written in 1773, well after Wade's time, doubtless represents the conditions he found when he first came to the Highlands:

> We found in the course of our journey the convenience of having disencumbered ourselves by laying aside what ever we could spare: for it is not to be imagined without experience how in climbing crags, and treading bogs, and winding through narrow and obstructed passages, a little bulk will hinder, and a little weight will burden.

In an effort to improve the situation and to get some work

---

[1] Only about one quarter of the total mileage of Military roads in the Highlands was built by Wade and some roads are incorrectly attributed to him.

on the roads started, a new act was passed by the Scottish parliament in 1669 making it obligatory for all tenants and cottars[2] to give six days work for three successive years and to provide for that period a horse and cart. Those who failed to give their labour were liable to have their goods seized. The new act was scarcely any more successful than the previous one. It was ill-considered, and little or no provision was made for the labourers' welfare. They were accustomed to working on the land, and knew nothing of road-making. Even with their good will, it is unlikely they would have been able to do much to improve the roads. John Knox describes one of these parties of unwilling conscripts in his book *A Tour through the Highlands of Scotland in 1786*. Though written much later, it is almost certainly applicable to of earlier attempts at communal road making.

At this time, the inhabitants of Sky were mostly engaged upon the roads in different parts of the island, under the inspection of the gentlemen and tackmen, and accompanied, each party, by the bagpiper. Many of these people had to travel eight miles from home, and the greatest part of them were at a loss for lodgings, excepting that which the cold earth and the open sky afforded. Yet, after all these labours and inconveniences, no effectual roads, and much less effectual bridges, can be made through these bogs and rocks, without the aid of the military and proper tools. A single company of soldiers, assisted by the country people, under the direction of an experienced overseer, would render the island more effectual service in one year, than all the unsupported exertions of the inhabitants can, in seven years.

In a determination to avoid giving labour, the practice grew of giving money equal to the number of days' work demanded— a labourer's daily rate at that time was about 3d. There were many tenants and cottars who neither provided the labour nor the money; but in any case, what was needed

---

[2] Cottar. 'A peasant who occupies a cottage belonging to a farm as a sort of out-servant.' (Oxford English Dictionary)

was not money but reliable and regular hard labour on the roads.

Not everyone, by any means, wanted the country opened up by a system of even the most primitive roads. For centuries the Highlands had been a land apart; the people were Celts, different from the lowland Scots whom they mistrusted and who with reason distrusted them. Organised cattle raids by the Highlands into the Lowlands were all too common. Towns were few, and apart from a few fishing communities in the more 'urban' coastal strip, the bulk of the population wrested a somewhat meagre living from the remote glens. They lived totally subject to the clan chief system which although hard, had in the past given them a certain amount of security and a place, however lowly, in their society. They knew nothing, and cared even less, of the dictates of an alien government ruling from Westminster. They lived together in small, widely scattered communities.

Again Knox paints a picture which we can recognise as very similar to the conditions that Wade found in the Highlands:

> Through a considerable part of the year, the inhabitants of each respective glen or valley may be considered as prisoners, strongly guarded by impassable mountains on one side, by swamps and furious torrents on the other. They disappear from public eye . . . Of the quality of the roads, it is hardly agreed upon by travellers which is the line of the road, everyone making one for himself. Even sheep follow better routes, understanding levels better and selecting better gradients. The common rate of travel being only one mile per hour.

The Highlanders were accustomed to this kind of life and their expectations of anything else were very limited. The men were ill educated, with a limited vision that extended very little beyond their own immediate needs, and the women knew only how to cook and how to rear a family. Their loyalties were to their chiefs through a series of lesser men— subtenants, tenants and tacksmen. In return for certain specified duties, they enjoyed the protection of their chiefs while they in turn had a ready-made army to protect them from neighbouring and often warring chiefs. Few of them had any desire to see the Highlands opened to anyone who could drive a horse and carriage. They were utterly opposed to any change, for they saw this as a threat to their own powers.

So it is little wonder that the Highlands lacked roads and that the Act authorising statute labour was so unsuccessful. But whether the chiefs liked it or not, change was coming. The activities of the Jacobites in England, the spasmodic outbreaks of rebellion in the Highlands and the unrest and in-fighting among the clans, forced the government to act.

The historical background

If, when she died in 1603, Elizabeth I had left a direct heir, the history of relations between England and Scotland would have been quite different; but she had none. The strongest claimant to the throne, the one she herself favoured, was her cousin, James VI of Scotland. His mother, Mary Queen of Scots, was the daughter of James V and the grand-daughter of James IV who married Margaret Tudor, Henry VIII's sister. Elizabeth was Henry's daughter by Anne Boleyn. James's claim was generally approved in England, and in due course he was crowned at Westminster, uniting for the first time two countries that had previously feuded for as many centuries as anyone could remember.

But this was a union only in as far as both countries had the same monarch. The Scottish parliament at Edinburgh and the English parliament at Westminster both continued in existence and this pattern persisted into the eighteenth century, except for the short period of the Commonwealth, 1649–60.

In 1688, however, relations were further complicated by the ousting of James VII and II by William and Mary in the 'Bloodless Revolution'. The right to the throne of William and Mary was variously viewed. To a majority, the practical advantages of being rid of James II were justification enough; but to a minority, both in England and Scotland, William and

Mary were merely usurpers. There seems little doubt that this latter view is the right one if the doctrine of the 'Divine Right of Kings' is accepted. We are indebted to Henry VII and the later Tudors for the initial 'promoting' of this doctrine; the succeeding Stuarts upheld it assiduously. Those whose consciences compelled them to acknowledge only James II and his heirs as kings became known as Jacobites, from the Latin form of James, Jacobus.

In 1707 an Act of Union was passed, both in Edinburgh and Westminster, which terminated the parliament in Edinburgh and brought 16 Scottish peers to the House of Lords and 45 members to the House of Commons, which already numbered over 500.

A glance at a map showing the physical geography of Scotland will reveal one more factor in the equation. North and west of a line running approximately from Aberdeen to Loch Lomond the country is mountainous; south and east of it, it is relatively flat. This lower area includes the two largest towns, Edinburgh and Glasgow. Contact with the south was always easier here, it was racially more mixed and the normal language was Scots. North and west of the line, in the mountainous area, the population was predominantly Celtic and Gaelic speaking.

This north-western part of Scotland had never been fully under the control of the Scottish government in Edinburgh and the change to a 'foreign' government four hundred miles further away did nothing to improve matters. The clans feuded with one another and regularly raided one another's cattle and sent marauding parties into the more prosperous lowland areas. This raiding has left a permanent mark in the English language in the word 'blackmail'. The word 'mail' means 'tribute' and the black tribute was the black cattle driven off by the raiders. Sometimes money was extorted from the farmers as the price of not having their cattle stolen, sometimes they managed to trace the location of their stolen cattle and succeeded in buying them back.

A Highlander's first allegiance was to his chief, and the chiefs often took little notice of the dictates of the Edinburgh parliament. The expulsion of James II and the removal of authority to a parliament in Westminster, where Scottish members were always in a small minority, could only have the effect of reducing still further their allegiance to the crown.

The first major uprising occurred in 1715, when the Earl of Mar, at the head of 15,000 Jacobite clansmen, attempted to recapture the throne for Prince James Edward, son of James II who had died in France in 1701. There were small sympathetic Jacobite risings in the north of England but the whole venture collapsed rather from poor leadership than defeat by Government forces. James Edward and Mar escaped to France.

In 1714, the year before the rising, Queen Anne had died and with her the Stuart line ended. The crown was offered to the Elector of Hanover, George I as he later became. This followed from the Act of Settlement of 1701 which determined that the House of Hanover should succeed if Queen Anne died without children. The link between the families came through George I's grandmother who was a daughter of James I.

It was this tangle of dynastic, cultural and political threads that the government was seeking to unravel in the years after the collapse of the 1715 rebellion. English troops were stationed at Inverlochy (now Fort William), Bernera in Glen Elg, Killichiumen (now Fort Augustus) and Ruthven, near Kingussie. They were greatly handicapped in their attempts to maintain the King's authority and in suppressing trouble-makers because they knew no Gaelic, so companies of Highland soldiers with Gaelic-speaking Highland officers were formed. As it proved difficult, in practice, to determine where their allegiance lay, they were disbanded in 1717.

The situation changed little until 1724, when Simon Fraser, Lord Lovat, sent a 'Memorial' to the Government, outlining the current state of affairs, and pointing out, truly, that the effect of recent decisions had been to handicap Highlanders loyal to the Government but not those hostile to it. He proposed more local companies, officered by Highland gentlemen of known loyalty.

George I and his advisers read this document but were not convinced of Lovat's integrity. They suspected he was seeking power for himself and his friends. Recognising the need for an independent report on the Highlands they called in Major-General George Wade.

General Wade

Wade's task in Scotland was to inspect in some detail 'the situation of the Highlanders, their manners, customs and the state of the country in regard to the depredations said to be committed in that part of His Majesty's domains...' and to suggest what needed to be done.

Just how far Wade penetrated into the Highlands in collecting information is not recorded. He spent five months on his highly competent report and he confirmed much of Lovat's Memorial. His recommendations included the re-establishment of the Highland Companies commanded by Highland officers and under martial law (he actually asked for six companies, three of sixty men and three of thirty men, armed and ready to join the regular troops), and the passing of a new Disarming Act which would include powers to implement it. In addition he proposed that two new forts should be built at Killichuimen and Inverness, that the barracks at Fort William should be repaired and that the roads—little more than footpaths connecting garrisons and barracks—should be greatly improved. He also proposed that a boat capable of carrying fifty–sixty soldiers and of supplying the new fort at Killichuimen should be built and available for use on Loch Ness. But the most important sentence from our point of view reads, 'the Highlands of Scotland are still more impracticable from the want of roads and bridges.'

His report produced immediate results and a fortnight later, on Christmas Eve, he was appointed commander of forces in North Britain, a position he held until 1740.

Wade's connection with Scotland was almost an accident and it is highly probable that if Lovat's Memorial had not been acted on and Wade had not been without a command at that moment, he would never have been sent there.

His subsequent years in the Highlands were perhaps his happiest. He was in sole command of his men and he was given a remarkably free hand by a government which had sufficient faith in his abilities.

Field Marshall George Wade was born in 1673, the third son of Jerome Wade of Kilavally, West Meath, whose father William Wade was a major of dragoons in Cromwell's army. It is for his roads that George Wade is remembered today, yet he was by training a soldier. His army career began on 26 December 1690 when he was appointed ensign to Captain R. Trevanion's company in the Earl of Bath's 10th Foot Regiment. It is said that he was at the Battle of Aughrim in Ireland in 1691, but this is unlikely as his regiment was in the Channel Islands in that year and later went to Flanders. He next served with his regiment at Steinkirk and was made Lieutenant in 1692–3. In 1695 he received an appointment as Captain of the Grenadier Company. He was sent to France where he apparently did well and he was promoted to Major in March 1703. From there in 1704 he went to Portugal with the brevet rank of Colonel and eventually moved on to Madrid.

In 1707–8 he was promoted to Brigadier General and returned to England in 1710. For the next four years his army life seems to have been uneventful and the next we hear of him is in October 1714 when he was promoted to Major General to serve in Ireland, although it is rather doubtful if he ever took up this appointment.

So in twenty-four years Wade had worked his way up from an ensign in the Earl of Bath's regiment to a Major General.

He became M.P. for Hinton in Wiltshire in 1714, a position he apparently held until 1722. After this he represented Bath for the rest of his life.

Bath and parts of the south-west were known to be strongly in sympathy with the Jacobite cause, and when the first major rebellion broke out in 1715 Wade was sent to Bath to prevent any risings occurring in the area. He had under his command two regiments of dragoons and he became very successful in ferreting out and foiling plots against the House of Hanover.

This campaign, although carried out entirely on English soil, seems to have been his first connection with Jacobitism and his success perhaps influenced the government in thinking him the right man to go to Scotland.

In June 1725 Wade arrived in Scotland and reached Inverness on 10 August. He started work immediately, confiscating arms, overseeing the training of the Highland Companies, building the boat and organising his soldiers for their work on the road, with buoyant enthusiasm.

From the beginning it was obvious that it was not sufficient to build forts and have fully trained soldiers placed at strategic points if they were unable to move around the country because of lack of roads. Wade put in another recommendation that a sum of money should be provided annually for road building and to pay the salary of an inspector whose duties it would be to examine the roads. This was the beginning. Work began on the roads in earnest in 1726. For the first time in the history of the Highlands there was money available in the hands of a man with drive and foresight and the network of roads linking the Highlands to the south was begun. Up to 500 soldiers were employed at a time and an unspecified number of civilians, chiefly skilled or semi-skilled craftsmen. So, at 51, Wade began on his secondary career. From his later reports it sometimes seemed as if he regarded road-making as his main work. He took great pleasure in being able to report the number of miles of road built each year.

He had taken on a tremendous job. He knew very little about road building or the nature of the countryside. He had yet to experience the devastation caused by heavy falls of snow or the force of the rivers in spate. He was working in what was virtually unmapped country and his labour force, although under military discipline was unskilled. He never made the mistake of undervaluing his men, his 'highwaymen' as he affectionately called them. Somehow or other he managed to persuade the government to increase their daily rate of pay for every day they worked on the roads and was continually fretting about the quality of their food, often bringing it up from Edinburgh at great expense. In 1727 Wade's service to the Highlands was duly acknowledged when he was promoted to Lieutenant General.

The reorganisation of the Highland Companies was not the immediate success he had hoped for. The chiefs viewed them with suspicion and would only hand over their arms to the regular army. The men were ill disciplined and in 1731, Wade had cause to complain that as soon as he left Scotland at the end of the summer, when work on the roads was impossible, they went home and did not return until they heard he was back again. He put them under tighter discipline, which was so successful that in 1732 when he was made governor of the three forts (Fort William, Fort Augustus and Fort George) he was able to report that they gave him every satisfaction. Seven years later in 1739, they were formed into a regular regiment to be known as the Black Watch on account of their dark neutral tartan.

After this, promotion again was rapid. He was made General in 1739, a privy councillor in 1742 and in 1743, three years after he left the Highlands, he was promoted Field Marshal. Later this year he was sent to Flanders as Commander of the British forces. Two years later, ill health compelled his return to England. When he was 72 he marched north seeking to put down the '45 rebellion. It was at this period that nightly audiences at Drury Lane commended him to God in the following verse added to the National Anthem, and sung, we are told, amid loud applause:

> God grant that Marshall Wade,
> May by thy mighty aid,
> Victory bring.
> May he sedition hush,
> And like a torrent rush,
> Rebellious Scots to crush,
> God save the King!

Unsuccessful in this his last command, he retired to private life. He died three years later at the age of 75, leaving two sons and two daughters and a fortune in excess of £100,000. He was unmarried.

In his will he left almost all his money to his children, but also included a sufficient provision for a monument for himself in Bath or Westminster. The monument was the work of the sculptor Roubiliac and was erected at Westminster. It is said that Roubiliac used to stand before what he described as 'his best work' and weep when he saw it had been placed too high to be fully appreciated.

The short term value of Wade's work in Scotland is hard to assess. He had gone to suppress rebellion, yet for some years after his departure there was still fighting. Although he reported his success at finding arms he was clearly not as successful as he thought. But to Wade must go the credit of being the first man to see that the problem in Scotland was the lack of any sort of communication and that until this was remedied there was very little chance of bringing peace to the country.

His former assistant and successor as road builder in the Highlands, William Caulfeild thought so highly of him that he named his son, Wade Toby after him. This tradition is still maintained in the Caulfeild family.

How the roads were built

As a road builder, Wade's task was to link the military bases in the Highlands and to join this road system to the Lowland roads. The bases were the three forts (Fort William, Fort Augustus, Fort George) along the Great Glen and the barracks at Ruthven near Kingussie. As far as making roads was concerned, the Great Glen was the northern boundary.

When Wade arrived in the Highlands, there were roads from the south finishing at Dunkeld and Crieff. The Dunkeld Road came via Perth from Edinburgh and the Crieff Road from Glasgow via Stirling. These were his southern starting points. His roads north from Dunkeld and Crieff joined at Dalnacardoch and this road continued to Inverness. From there his Great Glen Road ran south-west to Fort Augustus and Fort William and the last road, from Dalwhinnie on the Inverness Road, ran more or less directly to Fort Augustus.

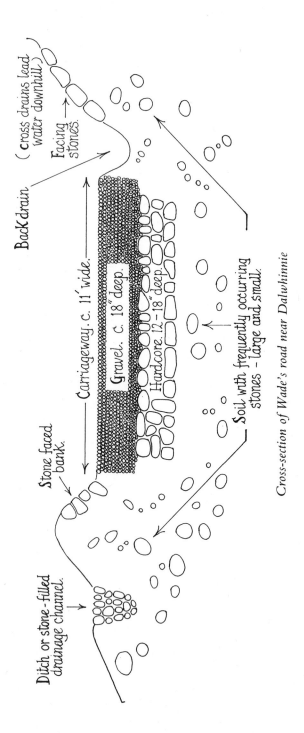

Back drain

(cross drains lead water downhill)

Facing stones.

Carriageway. c. 11' wide.

Gravel. c. 18" deep.

Hardcore. 12 - 18" deep.

Soil with frequently occurring stones - large and small.

Stone faced bank.

Ditch or stone-filled drainage channel.

Cross-section of Wade's road near Dalwhinnie

Altogether Wade built 250 miles of road between 1725 and 1732, and over a longer period 40 bridges. His two most famous bridges are the Aberfeldy bridge over the Tay and Highbridge over the Spean. Considering the difficulties he faced, the fact that his men were unskilled and that work could only be carried out for an average of seven months a year, this was remarkably quick. In reasonably good conditions, Wade and his Inspector Caulfeild were satisfied if a soldier completed one-and-a-half yards of road per day.

In every sense, Wade and his men were pioneers. There was nothing to build on; there were no maps or plans or specification for the kind of road needed. Furthermore, he could not invariably rely on the few local people supplying him with much-needed information. The usual procedure was to survey the land, making reference to burns, hills, rivers and marshy land and plan the route of the road during the summer, estimate the cost, and draw up the maps and plans. As these were made by amateurs, it is inevitable that mistakes were made. As a matter of interest, there are no records of landowners ever being consulted, or their permission sought before a road was built across their land or of compensation paid to them.

Wade left Scotland during the winter months, when work on the roads was impossible. While he was in England he presented his plans and estimated costs for the next summer to the government and reported on the work accomplished and in hand. No doubt he had a few battles with the Treasury before he received sufficient money for the next stage of his work. Although he had to account for every penny, including expenditure on medicines, it appears that his requests were met in full. On Wade's return to Scotland, usually in April, the advance party met Caulfeild and an engineer and work began.

The line of the road was staked out and marked with flags and camps were set up, usually every ten miles; these were either tents or huts. Finally the blacksmiths' forges for the repair of carts and implements were erected. The civilian craftsmen were engaged (they had their own rates of pay which had to be negotiated each year) and the soldiers were allocated their jobs, having previously handed in their arms.

Plainly the risk of their needing to defend themselves was thought to be slight.

Wade's working parties consisted of one captain, two subalterns, two sergeants, two corporals, up to 100 men, messengers and drummers. Their tools were simple: shovels, pickaxes, spades, iron crows, screw jacks and sledgehammers. They also had wheelbarrows and if there was rock to be blasted, gunpowder and fuses. All the materials they needed were at hand. Stones lay everywhere waiting to be used and practically every hill, when dug into, provided more than enough gravel. All that was needed was the horse and cart to transport it and this was usually provided by the Commissioners of Supply. Wade tried to keep his roads to a standard width of sixteen feet but in practice this varied, particularly when the roads were close to lochs or rivers or cut into steep hillsides.[3]

First the foundations were dug. For this the topsoil was dug out to form a trench, until a bed of stones was reached. The stones were levelled and if they were too big, they were levered out with screw jacks and crowbars, and if suitable were used as marker stones. Really big ones were split with gunpowder. Small stones broken down with sledgehammers were placed on top and levelled, and finally at least two feet of gravel was tipped on and and beaten in with shovels and feet. This gravel had to be renewed frequently. Marshy ground presented problems of a different nature. The road was dug out until, if they were lucky, firmer ground was reached. Where there was no firm ground a thick raft of brushwood and timber was placed in the trench and the road was built or floated on top. Through excessively boggy land, as an extreme measure, an embankment was built on top of the rafted road.

The earth from the trench was thrown on either side of the road to make banks. (These banks have helped identify many a doubtful Wade road today.) At the far side of each bank drainage channels were dug and where the road hugged a

---

[3] Some dimensions of today's roads for comparison: a two-lane 'A' road is about 26 feet, a 'B' road about 17 feet and a small unclassified country lane 10–11 feet.

hillside or loch a back drain was essential to prevent the road from being washed away. The problem was to get the water away from the back drain, the uphill side, so cross drains were built. These were made of stone and sunk a little way below the level of the top of the gravel.

When hills had to be climbed and the ascent was too steep to keep the road straight (as for example on the Corrieyairack), the road was built in a number of traverses or hairpin bends. This meant cutting the road out of the hillside, which then had to be supported by retaining walls of mortared stone. The last job was the placing of milestones and then the marker stones necessary to guide the traveller in the winter months. These, too, have helped identify Wade roads today.

Interesting evidence of the actual mode of construction of Wade's roads has come very recently from the civil engineers responsible for reconstructing the A9. During the course of their work they dug inspection trenches through the early roads at a number of points, and in some of these trenches located the original stone work of Wade's road under the later roads. They found that the carriageway varied in width from 10 feet 4 inches to 13 feet, considerably less than the 16 feet that Wade wanted. These measurements may represent the full width of the original road, but as we know from modern roads, deterioration occurs most rapidly at the edges and some width may have been lost in this way. In some cases, the bed of large stones put in by Wade's men can still be seen as a definite layer in the soil profile.

It is impossible to go very far anywhere in the Highlands without finding burns and rivers. Wherever possible Wade made a ford crossing. This had two obvious advantages. Firstly it was cheap to construct, needing no more work than was necessary to move the big loose stones and make a level bed of small ones. Secondly the road could then be used directly it was finished, without having to wait for the skilled craftsmen (who might not be immediately available), to build a bridge. Its disadvantage was that, during the winter, the additional water pouring off the hills dislodged the stones so that by the spring nothing remained of the ford and the work had to be done again. Eventually all but the smaller burns were bridged. But even these were to prove troublesome. The small peaceful burn, carefully surveyed in the summer, gave no indication of the raging torrent it became in the winter. Burt records the change in the character of one such small burn, and the fate of the bridge built over it.

> The spring of the arch was founded upon rocks, and it was elevated much above the highest water that had ever been known by the country-people; yet, some time after it was finished, there happened a sudden torrent from the mountains, which brought down trees and pieces of rocks; and, by its being placed too near the issue of water from between two hills, though firmly built with stone, it was cropt off, not far beneath the crown of the arch, as if it had neither weight nor solidity.

He comments philosophically . . . 'how short is human foresight, especially in new projects and untried undertakings.'

Wade also had social problems to cope with. His remarkably good relations with his men have been recorded many times but we know nothing of their feelings as they worked in the open, often in bleak tracts of land far from the security of their barracks and the routine of marching and drilling. Their evenings were enlivened by drinking and too often, after a heavy night, they were incapable of carrying out their duties. The trouble was there was nothing but spirits to drink. Years later, many an intrepid traveller complained of the lack of any drink but whisky.

Johnson, travelling with Boswell, amusingly illustrates Wade's problem. They met some soldiers working on the road to Bernera and having spent the previous evening agreeably at Fort Augustus,

> We begged leave to show our gratitude by a small present . . . In the evening the soldiers, whom we had passed on the road, came to spend at our inn the little money that we had given them. They had the true military impatience of coin in their pockets, and had marched at least six miles to find the first place where liquor could be bought. Having never been before in a place so wild and unfrequented, I was glad of their arrival, because I knew that we had made

friends, and to gain still more of their good will, we went to them, where they were carousing in the barn and added something to our former gift. All that we gave was not much, but it detained them in the barn, either merry or quarrelling, the whole night, and in the morning they went back to their work, with great indignation at the bad qualities of whisky.

The situation was not without its funny side. At Wade's suggestion, officers who were responsible for discipline, provided utensils and stores so that the men could brew their own beer. The Treasury heard of this and the officers concerned were ordered to attend the Court of Exchequer in Scotland to give an account of themselves. Wade asked for a stay of execution; nothing was settled and the dispute dragged on. In an effort to force an agreement, Wade ordered his men not to co-operate in their usual way with the excise officers—result, stalemate. It was eventually decided that:

> . . . the remote situation of the garrison, the unwholesomeness of the water, the spirits sold by the people of the country, the salt provisions, render it necessary for their health to provide good and wholesome drink. It is necessary to brew beer because of the heavy land carriage.

No doubt Wade wished that all his problems ended so satisfactorily.

As a Member of Parliament Wade was in the fortunate position of being able to report directly to the House. This must have been of inestimable value to him as he was able to plead his own case. Quite early on in his road-making career, Wade pointed out that roads do not last for ever and that regular maintenance was necessary. No clear-cut policy for maintaining the roads had been agreed and what repairs were done were ordered by Caulfeild and Wade. During his winter visits to London when Wade reported what extra work had to be done, he included in his estimate the cost of repairs. It was not until 1733, eight years after the commencement of his first road that he received a regular annual grant for maintenance.

The situation was far from satisfactory. By definition a

military road was a road for the use of the military and built by
them, although using civilian craftsmen—for specialists
jobs—paid for and maintained by the Treasury. But civilians
were never prevented from using the roads and by the end of
the eighteenth century, the volume of civilian traffic had
grown considerably. This increased the pressure for a much
more adequate road system throughout the Highlands and
caused a change of policy on the part of the government. As
the Highlands became more peaceful, the need for military
roads passed and the government looked for ways of ridding
itself of the expense of their upkeep. Statute labour had already
proved unsatisfactorily and at this time there was no way of
raising sufficient money from the landowners.

The annual expenditure on maintaining the roads was
meeting with growing hostility in Parliament, while those
concerned about the welfare and improvement of the
Highlanders viewed the future with growing dismay.
Without the roads, poverty and emigration could only
increase. Finally in 1790 all soldiers working on the roads were
withdrawn. From this year until 1814 parliamentary grants
continued, although little money was given and that with
reluctance. Maintenance was done, but now by civilian
contractors. An Act of 1810 empowered the Commissioners
of Supply to raise money for road maintenance from local
landowners, but this achieved nothing as the Act only
permitted action, it did not demand it.

Eventually in 1814 the maintenance of military roads was
made the responsibility of the Highland Roads and Bridges
Commission, set up under the Act of 1803 to oversee the
building of new roads in Scotland. At the same time the
Commission was made responsible for the maintenance of its
own new roads. The government made an annual grant of
£5000, the rest of the money had to be raised locally. At this
moment the Commissioners had some 1200 miles of road to
maintain and as maintenance averaged between £4 and £5 per
mile, the Treasury grant must have met most of the cost.

The Highland Roads and Bridges Commission continued to
be responsible for maintenance until 1862 when it was
disbanded. From then on, the responsibility rested with the

counties. Today little is being done to maintain the few remaining miles of Wade's roads not under tar, except where they are used as farm or forestry roads.

Practical considerations

There is nothing in the way of special equipment needed for these walks, none is very high or long and there are no dangers to be guarded against. But there are points worth remembering.

Footwear Most of these roads have damp patches, often there are very boggy stretches, and in addition there are plenty of burns to be forded, so a 'sensible pair of walking shoes' will only too quickly lead to soaked feet. Boots of some type are essential; some favour special walking boots, some prefer lace-up rubber boots, some swear by Wellingtons. There are people who wax remarkably fierce in defence of their own preferences and will allow no good in those of others. The only thing to do is to find what suits you. But do not buy an expensive pair of walking boots until you are certain that something much cheaper will not do you as well.

Another benefit from wearing boots is the protection they afford to the ankles against the scratching of old woody heather stems.

Clothing There is an unkind saying about Scottish weather: 'If you can see the hills it's going to rain; if you can't see them, it's raining.' This is an exaggeration of course, but rain *is* frequent among the hills and one needs to be prepared for it. Often it is very local but it is no consolation if you have been soaked in a downpour to be told afterwards that it was sunny in the next glen. Some form of *thoroughly* waterproof clothing is necessary, whether you prefer the jacket and trousers type or the Kagoul is a matter of taste. It is wise, too, to set off feeling somewhat too warm rather than the reverse; it is surprising how the temperature drops when you have climbed a few hundred feet.

Etceteras   If we expect to be walking for more than about an hour we always carry some food, usually chocolate and cakes, occasionally fruit. We never carry drinks; when you are really thirsty the burns taste like nectar and there is always one at hand. We also carry a compass and some sticking plaster. One of us never walks without a stick, a long one, the other finds no use for one. A small rucksack or haversack sometimes comes in handy.

Maps   Except for the very shortest sections, it is difficult to walk Wade's roads, where they diverge from today's without adequate maps. Even where it is possible, walking without a map deprives one of much interesting information. By far the most satisfactory maps to buy are the Ordnance Survey 1:50,000 series—about 1¼ inches to a mile. To cover all the Wade roads nine maps will be needed: sheets 26, 27, 34, 35, 36, 41, 42, 43 and 52. Below is a list of the maps needed for each road; they are listed in the order they are required.

> *Great Glen Road*   26, 35, 34, 41
> *Dunkeld to Inverness Road*   52, 43, 42, 35, 36, 27, 26
> *Crieff to Dalnacardoch Road*   52, 42
> *Dalwhinnie to Fort Augustus Road*   42, 35, 34
> *Link Road*   35

Because of the extensive changes it will be years before it is possible to buy an Ordnance Survey map showing the re-aligned A9 and its ancillary roads accurately, for maps are slow and very expensive to produce. However, where the map is out of date it will show the old road going through the towns and omit the later by-passes; this is the road usually needed. But remember the new road numbers will not appear.

Grid References   Whenever there is no other simple way of indicating a point on a map, a grid reference is given. Every Ordnance Survey sheet carries an explanation of how to calculate and interpret these references. It is very easy and no further explanation is given here. The six-figure grid reference, as used in this commentary, locates a point within a 100-km (approximately 60 miles) square. The longer grid references which locate a point anywhere within the British Isles have not been given as we do not feel them to be necessary.

The roads

The Great Glen Road from Inverness to Fort William—61 miles

This road was completed in the summer of 1727, when Wade drove from Inverness to Fort William in a coach and six, to the great astonishment of the population en route. With the completion of this road the three garrisons at Inverness, Fort Augustus and Fort William were directly connected for the first time.

Loch Ness looking south west from Dores. Wade's road (1732) hugs the south shore for several miles.

Wade's 1726 Road Inverness to Fort Augustus Sheet 1.

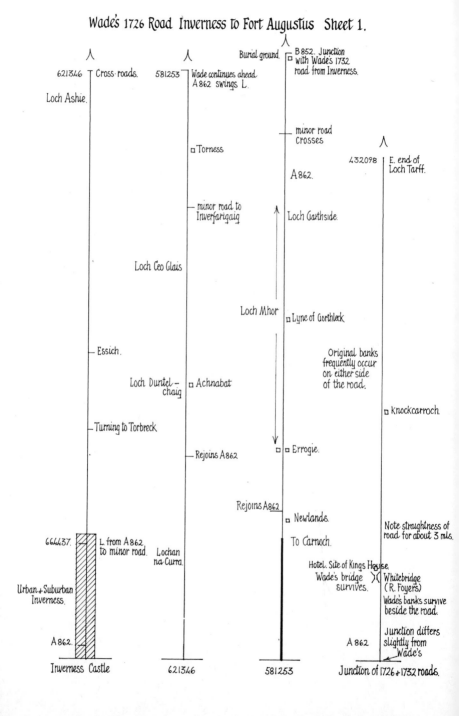

621346 Cross-roads.

Loch Ashie.

581253 Wade continues ahead A862 swings L.

Burial ground.

B852. Junction with Wade's 1732 road from Inverness.

minor road crosses

A862.

432098 E. end of Loch Tarff.

☐ Torness

minor road to Inverfarigaig

Loch Garthside.

Loch Ceo Glais

Loch Mhor

☐ Lyne of Gorthleck

Essich.

Original banks frequently occur on either side of the road.

Loch Duntel-chaig

☐ Achnabat

☐ Knockcarroch.

Turning to Torbreck

Rejoins A862

☐ ☐ Errogie.

Rejoins A862

☐ Newlands.

Note straightness of road for about 3 mls.

664437.   L. from A862 to minor road.

Lochan na Curra.

To Carnoch.

Hotel. Site of Kings House. Wade's bridge survives.

Whitebridge (R. Foyers)

Wade's banks survive beside the road.

Urban + Suburban Inverness.

A862.

Junction differs slightly from Wade's

A862.

Inverness Castle

621346

581253

Junction of 1726 + 1732 roads.

Inverness - Fort Augustus Road. Sheet 2
1726 road (completion) and 1732 road.

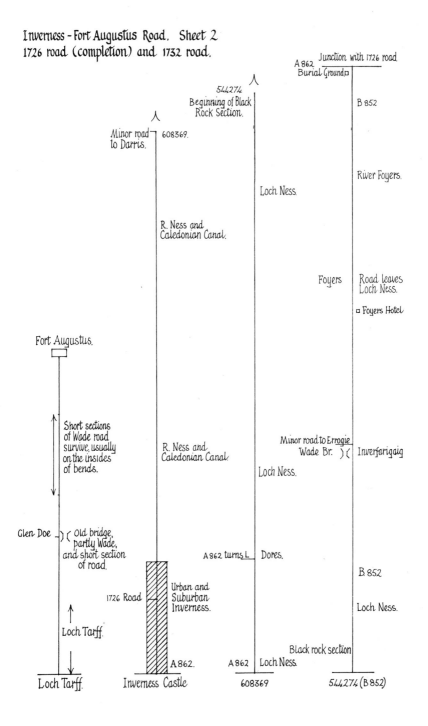

Fort Augustus.

Loch Tarff.

Short sections
of Wade road
survive, usually
on the insides
of bends.

Glen Doe ‑) (‑ Old bridge,
partly Wade,
and short section
of road.

Loch Tarff.

Loch Tarff.

Minor road
to Darris.

608369.

R. Ness and
Caledonian Canal.

R. Ness and
Caledonian Canal.

1726 Road

Urban and
Suburban
Inverness.

A862.

Inverness Castle

544274.
Beginning of Black
Rock Section.

Loch Ness.

Minor road to Errogie
Wade Br.) (‑ Inverfarigaig

Loch Ness.

A862 turns L   Dores.

A862   Loch Ness.

608369

A862 Junction with 1726 road.
Burial Ground□

B 852

River Foyers.

Foyers   Road leaves
Loch Ness.

□ Foyers Hotel

B 852

Loch Ness.

Black rock section

544274 (B 852)

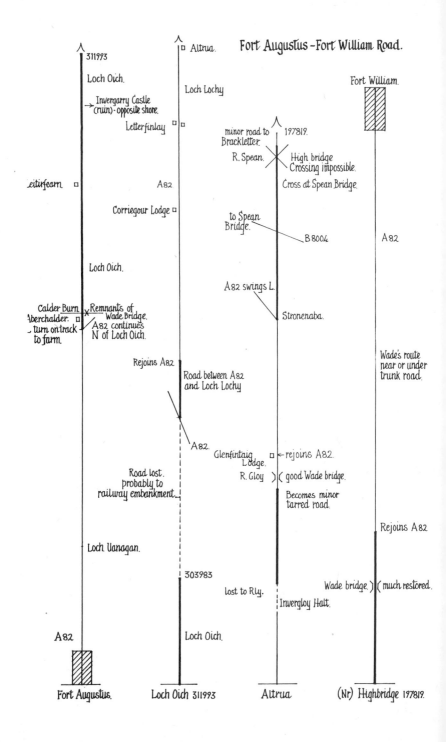

Fort Augustus - Fort William Road.

311993

Loch Oich.

→ Invergarry Castle (ruin) - opposite shore.

Altrua.

Loch Lochy

Fort William.

Letterfinlay

minor road to Brackletter.

197819.

R. Spean.

High bridge Crossing impossible.

Cross at Spean Bridge.

eitirfearn

A82

to Spean Bridge.

B 8004

A82

Corriegour Lodge

Loch Oich.

A82 swings L.

Stronenaba.

Calder Burn.
Aberchalder.
turn on track to farm.

x Remnants of Wade Bridge.
A82 continues N of Loch Oich.

Wade's route near or under trunk road.

Rejoins A82

Road between A82 and Loch Lochy

A82.

Glenfintaig Lodge.

← rejoins A82.

R. Gloy) (good Wade bridge.

Road lost. probably to railway embankment.

Becomes minor tarred road.

Rejoins A82

Loch Uanagan.

303983

lost to Rly.

Wade bridge.) (much restored.

Invergloy Halt.

A82

Loch Oich.

Fort Augustus.

Loch Oich 311993

Altrua

(Nr) Highbridge 197819.

Inverness to Fort Augustus

There are two roads over most of this route. The first road, built in 1726, was unsuitably sited and about two-thirds of it were replaced in 1732. Both are relatively quiet today as the main road, the A82, is north of Loch Ness. Both roads begin at Inverness Castle, on what is now the A862.

Peaceful Loch Duntelchaig.

1726 Road

About one mile after leaving the Castle, Wade's road turns left at 664437, onto the unnumbered minor road running south of Torbreck. This is a pleasant, narrow, twisting road, alternating between bleak moorland and afforestation. Several marker-stones still line the route; these were essential in snow when all other signs of the road were obliterated. The country here is not heavily settled and Essich is the only village the road passes through. It skirts Loch Ashie and then continues through woodland. There are two small lochs close to the road, Lochan na Curra and Lochan an Eoin Ruadha and behind them is Loch Duntelchaig. There is very little traffic on this road which makes it all the more pleasant.

At 598315 Wade's road rejoins the A862 and continues beside Loch Ceo Glais. Between the point where the A862 turns sharply left (an unnumbered minor road continues straight on to Inverfarigaig) and Lochgarthside (a place not a loch), at the far end of Loch Mhor, the route of Wade's road is uncertain. One possibility is that it continues along the minor road, through Bochruben, where there is an unusually tall and narrow bridge over a small burn, as far as Balchraggan. Here the route turns left along the forestry path and crosses the Farigaig. The bridge across the Farigaig is certainly not Wade's, although a few yards downstream are what could be the remains of an earlier bridge. From the bridge, the track goes on for half a mile and ends. If this is Wade's route, the section between the Farigaig and Lochgarthside has been lost.

A more likely route, which has the support of the most recent Ordnance Survey maps, follows the A862 until 851253, one-and-a-half miles beyond Torness and there continues along a two-mile stretch of minor road to Newlands (566229). This minor road has every sign of being Wade's: it is straight, with typical Wade banks built up and reinforced with stones, and there are what appear to be marker stones at intervals. At one time, this road must have been fairly settled for this part of the country, but now, alas, the crofts or small farms are in ruins, though the land is still farmed. The parallel section of the A862, in contrast, has hardly a house on it, suggesting that the minor road is very much the older of the two.

The 1726 road near Newlands.

After the turning to Carnoch, Wade's road, if it is his, has been tarred, but the stone-reinforced banks are still there. At Newlands there is a house with a garden directly in the line of the road, so it can be traced no further. It probably then continued beside Loch Mhor to Lochgarthside, much on the line of the A862.

About one-and-a-half miles beyond Loch Mhor, the B852 joins from the right. This is the Fort Augustus end of Wade's second, 1732 road from Inverness. The present junction of the two roads differs slightly from Wade's. There is an earlier bridge, 100 yards downstream of the present one, over the burn out of Loch Mhor. Wade most probably crossed here, initially perhaps by a ford. The route of his 1726 road to the old bridge and the junction with his 1732 road are still easy to pick out. After the bridge, his road swung left to resume the line of the A862.

At Whitebridge, Wade's bridge survives, although it is no longer in use. It is a few yards upstream of the present bridge and its approach roads can be plainly seen left of the A862. It is much restored and is said by the Inverness Field Club, which has put an informative notice about the bridge here, to be an outstanding example of a hump-backed bridge. It was built in 1732. The hotel nearby is on the site of a King's House.[4]

The next few miles of the A862 show plainly their origin as Wade's road, both by their straightness and by the survival for long stretches on one side or the other, of the typical stone-reinforced banks. These are most obvious just before Whitebridge. We know of nowhere else where these survive beside an 'A' road. The A862 runs over Wade's road right into Fort Augustus with only very minor variations. In some cases these can be seen as tracks beside the road but are hardly sufficiently long to warrant exploring. The most interesting is at 407088, a mile beyond Loch Tarff. Just before the present bridge, Wade's road leaves the tar, runs for a few yards downhill through grass to the Allt Doe. The bridge here is something of a puzzle as it is now a combination of two bridges. The smaller lower half (the downstream part) is obviously Wade. Butting on to this, at a higher level with a resulting ledge, is a later and wider part. It would seem that the wall of the original Wade bridge was knocked down and presumably what remains of it can now be seen as the ridge. This later bridge has a single arch in line with Wade's. Across

---

[4] King's House. The camps erected for the soldiers building the roads were in many cases later modified and became inns. They were built at ten-mile intervals and were called King's Houses because they were built on the King's Highway.

The Black rock section near Inverfarigaig.

the bridge, Wade's road is easily followed, through trees and overgrown scrub. It rejoins the A862, a little beyond the present bridge.

1732 Road

In this year, Wade replaced the major part of his road between Inverness and Fort Augustus by one close to the south side of Loch Ness. He had probably found that his earlier road was too exposed for winter use and was frequently blocked by snow. The advantage of this first road was that it was relatively easy and quick to construct. In contrast, the loch-side route involved blasting the road out of solid rock for a distance of over a mile. By 1732 Wade and his 'highwaymen' were much more experienced and skilled road makers and were better able to tackle this major undertaking. Even with modern machinery and explosives, cutting this route would be far from easy.

From the Castle, Wade's road runs along the A862 as far as Dores. So far the road has relatively little to offer by way of interest. At Dores, Wade continues straight on, taking the B852 along the side of Loch Ness. This loch, in its deep rift through the Scottish mountains, is impressive at any time of the day or of the year, and driving along this relatively unfrequented road is a good way to see it. The B852 is a single-track road but there are plenty of passing-places where one can pause awhile, provided your car does not obstruct.

About three miles before Inverfarigaig, the road enters the section hewn out of the rock. Wade called this the 'Black Rock' section, though the rock is dark grey rather than black. It was removed by blasting with gunpowder, a long, laborious and often dangerous job. It has to be remembered that all the holes for the charges of gunpowder had to be made with hammers and chisels. Then the gunpowder was packed in by hand, a fuse was added and lighted and the soldiers hurriedly retreated to what they hoped was a safe distance. When the rumbles were over and the dust had settled, all the fallen rock had to be collected and carted away. Most of it, no doubt, finished up in Loch Ness. As the loch is deeper than the North Sea there was little danger of the rubble making shallows. There seems to have been no extra danger-money paid for this work and we have no records of any protective clothing. If there were any casualties they have not been recorded.

The Black Rock section does not present today's motorist with any cause for apprehension as the road is practically level and of ample width. To envisage it as it was in 1732, imagine the road only seven to eight feet wide, with gradients of up to one in five and a considerable drop down to the water on the outside. Parapet walls were put in to reassure nervous travellers but only at the most dangerous parts. The Great Glen, running south-west to north-east, is directly in line with our two strongest winds and the steep hills on each side funnel them into particularly furious blasts. These could well blow a carriage over, and in the Black Rock section, this was no trivial matter. All this was probably known to Wade and could well have been taken into consideration in the siting of his first road. Winds along the loch can still be so ferocious that there are times when present-day boatmen will not sail, despite their powerful modern boats.

Fortunately we have an eye-witness account of the making of this part of the 1732 road from 'A Gentleman Residing in the North of Scotland', thought to be Edward Burt. He was stationed at Inverness and travelled extensively in the Highlands in the 1720s and '30s. The account appears in a series of letters written to a friend in southern England. Burt appears to have been an acute observer and generally in sympathy with the Scots. The 'miners' referred to were the equivalent of today's Royal Engineers and they specialised in demolitions with explosives:

It is quite a scramble to reach this viewpoint of Inverfarigaig bridge.

The spectacular Falls of Foyers.

There the miners hung by ropes from the precipice over the water (like Shakespear's gatherers of samphire from Dover Cliffs) to bore stone, in order to blow away a necessary part from the face of it, and the rest likewise was chiefly done by gunpowder; but, when any part was fit to be left as it was, being flat and smooth, it was brought to a roughness proper to a stay to the feet; and, in this part, and all the rest of the road, where the precipices were like to give horror or uneasiness to such as might pass over them in carriages, though at a good distance from them, they are secured to the lake-side by walls, either left in the working or built up with stone, to a height proportioned to the occasion.

After the Black Rock, the road goes through Inverfarigaig. Wade's bridge across the river here can be seen upstream of the present one. It is perfectly possible to drive across this new bridge without being aware that it is a bridge at all, as it is surmounted by an embankment. Until a decade or two ago, Wade's bridge was still in use. The approach roads to it have been eliminated in building the new embanked road but it is still possible to scramble down through the undergrowth to reach it.

The road continues pleasantly along the loch side until Foyers and then turns inland. In the vicinity of the two churches to be found at the far end of Foyers, Wade had one of his 'Hutts' that he occupied while superintending the building of the road. No traces of it remain, as it was probably a temporary building with walls of turf and wood and a thatched roof. After two or three miles the road joins the A862 which here is on the line of Wade's 1726 road and the re-routing is complete.

Of the two roads, the higher 1726 road is the more interesting, at least we thought so. It also looks more like a Wade road. These roads from Inverness to Fort Augustus are unique among the Wade roads in being the only ones almost entirely under tar today.

Looking northward towards Loch Ness from Foyers gorge.

Wade's road skirts the south shore of Loch Tarff.

Fort Augustus to Fort William

Very little of eighteenth-century Fort Augustus remains; what does is incorporated in the buildings of the Benedictine Abbey. Wade's road coincides with the A82 from Fort Augustus to Aberchalder. Here the A82 turns right to cross to the north side of Loch Oich. Before the bridge over the Caledonian Canal, Wade's road turns left, (signposted to 'Aberchalder Farm'), and carries on over the Calder Burn. Here, until comparatively recently, there was a Wade bridge. Today very little of it remains, although it is obvious where it was. There is a replacement bridge beside it. Over the bridge, the Wade road continues as a grassy path along the edge of Loch Oich for about four miles. Compared to most of Wade's

Locks on the Caledonian canal at Fort Augustus.

roads, there is almost a suburban feel about this one. The only difficulties, and these are slight ones, occur in places where the bank has been eroded, taking the path with it. There are some overgrown, scrubby areas and on occasions fallen trees block the path, but there is always an easy way round.

It would seem that this road is often walked, a good place to exercise the dog on Sunday. Small burns find their way down from the hills into the loch, but they can be crossed without trouble. It is not easy to walk these roads without thinking of Wade's men and their difficulties, pleasures and small satisfactions. Perhaps they swam in the loch or dangled their hot tired feet in the water to cool them or drank avidly from the burns.

At the south end of Loch Oich, Wade's road is probably on the line of the disused railway (today only the embankment remains), until it reaches the A82, the exact line being hard to determine. Near the north end of Loch Lochy and shortly after the turning to the Laggan Lochs, Wade's road runs between the loch and the A82 for three-quarters of a mile. The first part, immediately beside the A82, is difficult to see and very overgrown. It then goes through cleared forestry before joining the A82 at 820949. From here it follows the loch and the A82 for five miles. It then turns left, but the first few yards of the road have been lost to the railway and to the station buildings, now the Invergloy Halt Guest House. Unfortunately the only approach to Wade's road is through the grounds and to the back of the guest house. From here, it can be seen climbing steeply parallel to the A82 and above it on the hillside. It drops down to the River Gloy which it crosses by Low Bridge, a much renovated Wade bridge, then turns right and rejoins the A82 at Glenfintaig Lodge, two miles from

The road alongside Loch Oich.

Low Bridge over the Gloy.

the point at which it left it. Today the A82 crosses the River
Gloy a mile downstream of Low Bridge and follows a flatter,
easier route by the river. Presumably Wade avoided this route
because it was then too swampy to be usable.

From Glenfintaig Lodge Wade's road continues along the
A82 to Stronenaba where, just before the AA box (208845), it
swings right. Initially the road is good enough for a car, but,
after a quarter of a mile, it becomes a damp path through
forestry and emerges after one mile to run briefly along the
B8004. There is nothing to suggest, visually, that this stretch
from Stronenaba to the B8004 is Wade's road, but from the
evidence of the best of the eighteenth-century maps and from
the very Wade-like nature of the road soon after it leaves the
B8004, there seems no reason to doubt that it is his route.
Presumably the road through the forestry was widened, so

destroying Wade's road-work, before the conifers were planted. There is a fence without a gate where it joins the B8004, and after a few yards, Wade's road leaves again, through a gate to the right. The last section in the forestry, the section along the B8004 and the section to the right of it are all in a straight line, suggestive of a road older both than the forestry and the B8004.

After leaving this road, Wade's road goes through rough, heathery grazing; soon the characteristic stone-reinforced banks appear and there are occasional marker stones. At the far end of this rough grazing, there is a gate leading to the riverside woodland. After the gate, Wade's road goes on descending through scrub, whereas the more obvious path swings left and climbs. Very shortly Wade turns left, and as the road is much overgrown, it is not easy to see. It runs steadily downhill and its exact line is sometimes a matter of conjecture but the general direction is clear enough. When the road begins to level out, there is a small burn with clear evidence of a stone bridge. The broken remains of slabs of stone still lying there are probably parts of the ones that carried Wade's road across the burn. Just below and to the right is the route of the former Spean Bridge to Fort Augustus railway, easily recognisable for what it is. Wade's road runs obliquely across this shortly after crossing the burn and curves away to its right, directly to Highbridge. Most fortunately for Wade-road hunters, there is a fallen brick chimney-stack from a railway hut just in line with the end of the bridge, for, particularly when the trees are in leaf, it is possible to walk right past it without seeing it, even though it is less than 50 yards away. We know that Highbridge was not built until 1736, but Wade says he drove along this route in 1727, nine years earlier. How and where he crossed the Spean remains a matter for speculation.

Highbridge is 280-feet long and had three arches. Two have now fallen and the third is badly cracked, but the two massive columns, over 60 feet high, still rise impressively from the river. Unlike the Tay bridge, it is built of rubble. At some period a lattice-work footbridge has been put across the columns and its rusting remains survive from the east bank to

Near Spean Bridge can be seen this well known memorial to the Commandos who trained nearby for action in the last War.

the second column. Even in its ruins it is a very impressive and somewhat awesome sight.

As it is impossible to cross the Spean by Highbridge, re-trace the route to the B8004 and continue along it until it joins the A82.[5] Follow the road through to Spean Bridge and on in the direction of Fort William. One mile beyond the bridge is a small turning to the right marked 'Brackletter and Highbridge'. Take this turning, and less than a mile down, by the first house on the right, there is a notice giving directions to the bridge and brief details of it. The route from the road to the bridge, though short, is wet in places, but the latter part is plainly a Wade road. A few yards before the bridge there is a rough track on the right which leads down to river-level. There is a great feeling of cut-offness there by the river, with the towering ruins of the massive bridge above. Except for the rush of waters over the boulders all is very silent and remote.

For the next section of Wade's road to Fort William, return to the minor road to Brackletter. After the house, the road runs straight for 200 yards and then turns sharply right. This 200 yards section is on Wade's road and it continues straight ahead when the Brackletter road turns right. Again this is very muddy going. Part of the road runs beside a wall and so is easily followed. There are occasional marker stones and several burns to cross but these are not difficult. The one Wade bridge surviving has been heavily repaired but the stone-work of the approaches seems to be little changed.

After about two miles, land improvement makes the Wade road hard to locate but there is a track, probably not his route, which leads on to the A82. From here to Fort William itself there is very little sign of Wade. The site of the Fort is now occupied by the railway and the only part of the building to survive, the gateway, has been moved and now marks the entrance to a cemetery.

---

[5] The Commando Memorial here is an impressive tribute to the commandos in the 1939–45 war, many of whom were trained in this area.

The road from Dunkeld to Inverness— 102½ miles

The overall direction of this road is north, but it winds so extensively to avoid the most mountainous areas that at times one is travelling almost due east, at others almost due west when making for Inverness. We have thought it simplest to describe travel in the direction of Inverness as 'north' and consequently the 'east' side of the road is always the right hand one and the 'west' the left hand one.

This road was the main line of communication in Wade's road system; it was built in 1728–9 and linked Edinburgh to Inverness. Later road engineers have, in general, kept to Wade's route and his road is the forerunner of today's A9. Improvements to the A9 have been particularly extensive of recent years but the process is nearly complete. These roadworks present their problems. The improvements are in some cases built on top of, or very close to the old A9 (substantially Wade's route), and in other cases diverge quite widely from it. Where the new road diverges, the old road becomes a minor one. It is often this old road that is needed and where the new numbers have been allocated we give them. Ironically, Wade and his men completed the major part of this road in about eighteen months. The present road works have already lasted for years.

Wade did not consider bridging the Tay at Dunkeld, this had to wait for Telford, who built the present elegant bridge in 1809. The existing road from Edinburgh via Perth ended at Inver, half a mile upstream from the present bridge, where there was a ferry for wheeled traffic as well as passengers and their equipment. Signs of what may be the ferry moorings can be seen on both sides of the river. As the Tay here is swift and wide there must have been times when the crossing was hazardous, perhaps impossible.

Dunkeld-Inverness Road
Sheet 1.

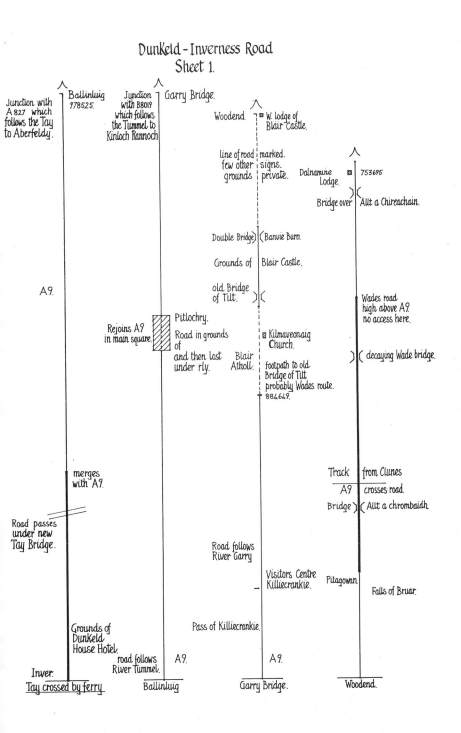

Junction with A 827 which follows the Tay to Aberfeldy.

Ballinluig 978525.

Junction with B8019 which follows the Tummel to Kinloch Rannoch

Garry Bridge.

Woodend.

W. lodge of Blair Castle.

line of road marked. few other signs. grounds private.

Dalnamine Lodge. 753695

Bridge over Allt a Chireachain.

Double Bridge) (Banvie Burn.

Grounds of Blair Castle.

A9.

old Bridge of Tilt.

Wades road high above A9 no access here.

Rejoins A9 in main square.

Pitlochry.

Road in grounds of and then lost under rly.

Kilmaveonaig Church.

Blair Atholl.

footpath to old Bridge of Tilt probably Wades route. 884649.

decaying Wade bridge.

merges with A9.

Track from Clunes

A9 crosses road.

Bridge) (Allt a chrombaidh

Road passes under new Tay Bridge.

Road follows River Garry

Visitors Centre Killiecrankie.

Pitagowan

Falls of Bruar.

Pass of Killiecrankie.

Grounds of Dunkeld House Hotel.

road follows River Tummel.

A9.

A9.

Inver. Tay crossed by ferry

Ballinluig

Garry Bridge.

Woodend.

Dunkeld - Inverness Road.
Sheet 2.

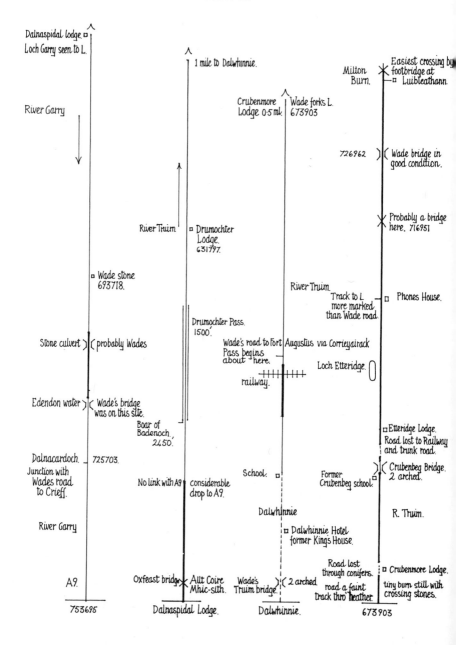

Dalnaspidal lodge.
Loch Garry seen to L.

River Garry

1 mile to Dalwhinnie.

Milton Burn.

Easiest crossing by footbridge at Luibleathann.

Crubenmore Lodge. 0·5 ml.

Wade forks L. 673903

726962 Wade bridge in good condition.

River Thuim

Drumochter Lodge. 631797.

Probably a bridge here. 716951

Wade stone 693718.

River Thuim.

Track to L more marked than Wade road.

Phones House.

Drumochter Pass. 1500'

Stone culvert probably Wades

Wade's road to Fort Augustus via Corrieyairack Pass begins about here.

Loch Etteridge.

railway.

Edendon water Wade's bridge was on this site.

Boar of Badenoch. 2450.

Etteridge Lodge.
Road lost to Railway and trunk road.

Dalnacardoch. 725703.
Junction with Wades road to Crieff.

No link with A9 considerable drop to A9.

School.

Former Crubenbeg school.

Crubenbeg Bridge. 2 arched.

River Garry

Dalwhinnie

R. Thuim.

Dalwhinnie Hotel former Kings House.

A9.

Oxfeast bridge Allt Coire Mhic-sith.

Wade's Thuim bridge.

2 arched

Road lost through conifers. road a faint track thro' heather.

Crubenmore Lodge. tiny burn still with crossing stones.

753695

Dalnaspidal Lodge.

Dalwhinnie.

673903

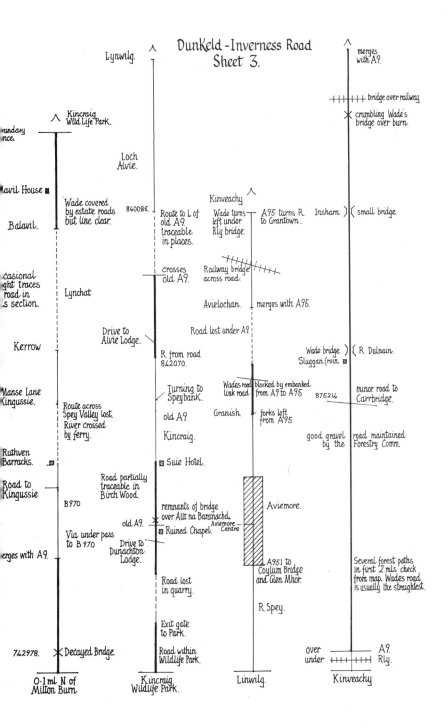

DunKeld - Inverness Road.
Sheet 4

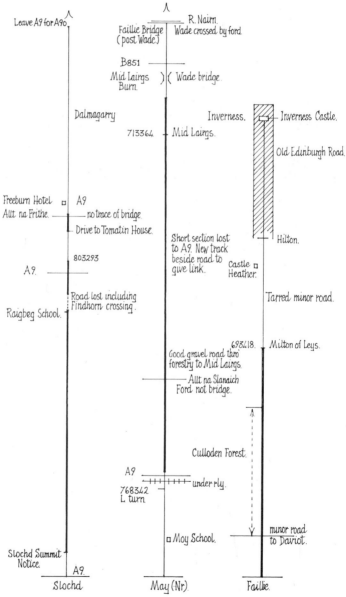

Leave A9 for A90

Faillie Bridge
(post Wade.)

R. Nairn.
Wade crossed by ford.

B851

Mid Lairgs
Burn.

)(Wade bridge.

Dalmagarry

713364 — Mid Lairgs.

Inverness.

Inverness Castle.

Old Edinburgh Road.

Freeburn Hotel · A9
Allt na Frithe. — no trace of bridge.
— Drive to Tomatin House.

Short section lost
to A9. New track
beside road to
give link.

Castle
Heather.

Hilton.

803293

A9.

Tarred minor road.

Road lost including
Findhorn crossing.

Raigbeg School.

693418. — Milton of Leys.

Good gravel road thro'
forestry to Mid Lairgs.

— Allt na Slanaich
Ford not bridge.

Culloden Forest.

A9
768342
L. turn.

under rly.

Moy School.

minor road
to Daviot.

Slochd Summit
Notice.
A9.

Slochd

May (Nr).

Faillie.

Frosted birch trees beneath Craigiebarns at Dunkeld.

Wade's road begins from the north end of the ferry and follows the east bank of the Tay through what are now the grounds of Dunkeld House Hotel. Dunkeld House was formerly the home of the Dukes of Athol, and the grounds contain some fine specimens of rare conifers. A short stretch of about two miles of road never far from the river has survived. In parts it is not much more than a path and is rather overgrown, necessitating much bending under tree branches. For most of the way there are remnants of a stone retaining wall on the uphill side. As the road climbs there is a wooded drop down to the river and several fishermen's paths branch off. It is a delightful walk, one to linger over and, for a Wade road, remarkably dry; it is easy to forget that the A9 is so near.

After the woodland, the road passes under a new bridge

A short section of Wade's road is visible between the new road and the river.

carrying the A9 over the Tay, and Wade's road has been resurfaced for the lorries carrying materials for road building, giving it a new lease of life. Here, three roads to the Highlands can be seen side by side. First, and by far the most interesting is the Wade road, then, next to it the A9 and further uphill, the one which was itself the A9 until the new road was built. So the road that replaced Wade's road has itself been replaced. Within a few hundred yards all three have merged.

The A9 now by-passes Pitlochry and will eventually by-pass Killiecrankie, Blair Atholl and Calvine, so it is important to stay on what was the A9—as yet unnumbered—which roughly follows the line of Wade's road. Two miles north of the junction of the A827 to Aberfeldy, an unclassified minor road signed to East Haugh and Dalcapon leaves on the right. Bear left almost immediately and you are back on the line of Wade's road. After one and a half miles, the road becomes the A924 to Pitlochry. From now on until beyond Pitlochry there

The Pass of Killicrankie.

are only slight traces of Wade's road; the drive to Dundarroch Hotel, for example, is on the line of his road. Half a mile north of Pitlochry, the road rejoins the A9.

There is a short section of Wade's road at the north end of the National Trust for Scotland's Information Centre at Killiecrankie. It can be traced as a grass track as far as the village hall. As a matter of interest, the trooper called McBean who made the famous soldier's leap at the Battle of Killiecrankie in 1689, is reputed to have assisted in the building of Wade's road.[6]

Through Blair Atholl, the route is uncertain, largely because of the landscaping of the extensive grounds surrounding Blair Castle. In the process almost all the signs of Wade's roads have been removed.

---

[6] A few yards of Wade's road has recently been discovered by Mr N. A. Reid of the NTS surviving beneath the tarmac of another road, just above the burn at the south end of the NTS car park.

He crossed the Tilt by the Old Bridge of Tilt, where a bridge had existed since the sixteenth-century. It is half a mile upstream of the bridge carrying the A9. He may have reached this bridge along the line of the path swinging right from the A9 at 884649, passing in front of Kilmaveonaig. Bridges were extremely rare in the areas of Scotland in which Wade was working, and where one occurred on the line of his road, he would naturally make use of it. The present bridge on the site of the Old Bridge of Tilt is *not* old, it has only been there for a few years; but underneath it can be seen the masonry that supported earlier bridges.

After the Tilt, he probably took the direct route to St Bride's church at Old Blair, carrying straight on where the tarred road now forks right, and crossed the Banvie Burn at the same place as at present. There is an odd 'two-tier' bridge over the burn. A second bridge has been built on an embankment on top of the first one, in order to avoid the steep descents to the old lower bridge. It is still possible to cross on a footpath at the level of the lower bridge. It is obviously old, probably eighteenth-century, but whether it is Wade's or not is impossible to say.

When, shortly after the bridge, the road ends at a T-junction, the route of Wade's road is said to be preserved in the line of trees that continues on across the field. Thereafter it passed close to Woodend and descended to the line of the A9 in the vicinity of the West Lodge. This last part, from the T-junction, is not within the area of the Castle grounds to which there is public access.

The next section diverges from the A9 at Pitagowan. In the woodland past the Falls of Bruar Hotel, there is, according to the Ordnance Survey map, a path leading to a tunnel under the railway, at the west end of the wood. This path seems to have disappeared but it is not difficult to find the tunnel. At its far end a gate in a deer fence leads to Wade's road, running left, up hill and roughly parallel to the A9, but it is not very obvious. There is a small coppice one-third of a mile on and the road runs along the north side of it; as here the road is plain, this can serve as a marker.

At the far end of the coppice, Wade's road crosses the

Blair Castle.

The Falls of Bruar.

Minigaig Pass road from Blair Atholl to Ruthven. This is centuries older than Wade's and is said to have been used by his soldiers as a short cut to and from Ruthven Barracks. Wade's road then continues for another three miles until it reaches the A9 again. This section is easy to follow and if the road by the railway tunnel is missed, a simpler starting place for this part is the Minigaig Pass road. This leaves the A9 in the centre of Calvine, opposite the turning to Kinloch Rannoch (B847) and is plainly signed. A steep climb for a quarter of a mile leads to the point where Wade's road crosses. It goes through open moorland with fine hills in view to the left, then through forestry to a well-preserved one-arched bridge over the Allt-a-Chrombaidh. Like many other bridges this was built on rock rising from the river bed. Shortly after the forestry has ended, the road crosses a well-defined, wide path which runs from Clunes Lodge across the A9 into the hills. Wade's road leads straight to a large, walled sheep-enclosure. It is easier to leave Wade and go round the uphill edge of the enclosure and rejoin him at the other side. There is no mistaking the road; it is marked by walled banks or their remains. When these end, it goes through a birch wood to cross an unnamed burn where there is an engaging remnant of a Wade bridge. This is not immediately recognised as a bridge as it has no parapets, and there is a sizeable tree growing from the top of the arch, its roots twined round the stones, probably holding them together. Like so many burns in this area, this has carved a deep channel and the bed is solid rock, a delightful spot for a picnic. Over the bridge, the road drops gently and there is a further half a mile or so until it ends abruptly at a fence, below which is the A9. No access is possible, and there is no alternative but to go back either to the Clunes Lodge path or further back to the Minigaig Pass road.

The next point of interest is the Wade bridge over the Allt-a-Chireachain by Dalnamine Lodge. This is on the right of the A9. The bridge is well preserved and there are short sections of the approach road each side of it. Two miles further north is Edendon Bridge. After the bridge there is nearly one mile of Wade road to the right. The A9 here is dual carriageway, with the two carriageways well separated. It is impossible to reach this short section of Wade road from the north-bound carriageway. From north to south, Wade's road begins at a gate at 703713 and ends at another at 714708. These gates have been put in by the road engineers solely to give

The Wade Stone.

access to his road. There is a stone culvert, probably Wade's over the first burn. Wade's bridge over the Edendon Water was on the same site as the bridge on the north-bound carriageway.

One-and-a-half miles north of the bridge is the Wade Stone. It is also on the east side of the road and again is best approached from the south-bound carriageway. It is eight feet high and was one of the marker stones on the original Wade road. The story is told that to amuse himself Wade, who must have been a tall man, reached up and put a guinea on the top, presumably when no one was watching. When he returned the following year he found his guinea still there. It is from this incident that the stone has acquired its name. With the construction of the new A9 the stone had to be moved as it would have been in the middle of the north-bound carriageway. It has been moved with great care to its present position beside the new south-bound carriageway as near as possible to its original location. The road engineers went to great trouble to see that the re-erecting was accurately accomplished. The stone is buried in the earth to just the same depth and the smaller stones by it were sketched in situ and numbered before removal so that they could be replaced in the same position relative to the Wade Stone. There is a good deal of carving on the stone but only the date 1729 is original.

The next separation of the A9 and Wade's road is for about one-and-a-half miles in the vicinity of Dalnaspidal Lodge. Wade's road is on the east. A car can be left in a lay-by to the west of the road. The gate giving access to the road is a short distance north of the A9 bridge over the Allt Coire Mhic-Sith. All traces of Wade's bridge over the burn have long gone; it was a few yards above the present one. But slight indications of the road on the far side of the burn are to be seen.

The lost bridge was known as 'Oxbridge' as the soldiers held a feast here in October 1729 to celebrate the completion of the road. They roasted four oxen whole and invited their general to be their guest, one more indication of his excellent relations with them. It must have been quite a party because he reported in a letter to a friend that he was on his feet again in a day or two!

From the gate Wade's road goes uphill and swings left to run parallel to and above the A9. (As the road swings left another similar road comes in on the right. We shall refer to this later.) After the swing left, Wade's road is easily followed through the heather. It finishes at a fence but access to the A9 has not been provided as it is some way below. The road coming in from the right which we referred to above went to the bridge that replaced Wade's. A little of its masonry remains and the road, like Wade's, can be traced across the burn, running back to the A9. This replacement bridge probably dates from the latter part of the eighteenth century.

The road then goes through the Drumochter Pass between

The partially snow covered hills above Drumochter Pass. Wade's road crosses from left to right in the middle distance.

Dalwhinnie. Wade's bridge across the Truim.

peaks rising above 2000 feet. This is some of the bleakest and most forbidding country traversed by a Wade road. Interestingly, the new A9 which is above the Wade road, which for so many years was the A9, makes the pass feel less claustrophobic and oppressive.[7]

At the point where the A889 leaves the A9, above one mile south of Dalwhinnie, Wade crossed the Truim and his two-arched bridge still stands, but there is no trace of the road on

---

[7] In choosing to take his road across the Drumochter Pass Wade added considerably to its length. There are more direct routes between Blair and Ruthven to the east of Drumochter, using either the Gaick or Minigaig Passes, and tracks, making use of both of them, existed long before his time. The problem is that both passes are about 1000 feet higher than Drumochter and are blocked with snow for longer periods in the winter. It is presumably for this reason that he avoided them. A century later, Telford and Mitchell looked at the problem again, in an attempt to eliminate this detour through Drumochter but they too decided that the shorter routes to the east were too high to be used.

the far side. It went, apparently straight to Dalwhinnie School
but later developments, particularly the building of the
railway have obliterated all traces of it. It continues north,
west of the Truim along the old A9, now an unclassified minor
road. But before this, at the north end of the village there is one
short section of Wade's road surviving. Where the A889
swings left, the Wade road goes straight on (641857) and is cut
by the railway before rejoining the road after about half a mile.
Wade's road linking Fort Augustus directly with the south via
the Corrieyairack Pass joined the Dunkeld to Inverness road
somewhere in this area, although it is not possible to
determine exactly where.

His road and the unclassified minor road (the old A9)
coincide until 673902 about half a mile south of Crubenmore
Lodge, where Wade forks left. The beginning of the road is
very hard to pick out as it is very little more than two indistinct
ridges through rough vegetation. If the beginning is missed, it
can be found more easily in the vicinity of the milestone 250
yards north (Newtonmore six miles). It is much plainer here
and is about 50 yards uphill and west of the present road. It
then runs behind a small hillock and continues on to the
plantation surrounding Crubenmore Lodge.[8] Just before the
plantation it crosses a tiny unnamed burn flowing into the
Truim. In the burn are several flat stones jammed together to
make a crossing. These may well be the original crossing
stones, as this route was not in use for very long.

The road is non-existent through the plantation but it is
open enough to walk through without undue difficulty. It
passes west of the farm house behind Crubenmore Lodge,
goes through a gate and is then easily followed to the old
Crubenbeg school, now a farm. Here it swings right to go
over the Falls of Truim by a two-arched bridge.

Over the bridge, the road swings left then just when it turns

---

[8] From Crubenmore Bridge on the now unclassified road a much older
bridge can be seen upstream crossing the Truim. This is not a Wade bridge
but was part of a late eighteenth-century re-routing of Wade's road. On the
east side, the road now disappears under the railway track.

In the vicinity of Ruthven barracks.

slightly right, Wade's road goes straight on through a field and disappears under the railway and the A9, old and new. On the far side of the roads and also of the Etteridge arable land adjacent to them, his road can be seen again running uphill in front of Etteridge Lodge. From here on, there is a pleasant six-mile stretch of walkable road, the last leg of the road to Ruthven Barracks.

The most convenient approach to this road is from the farm road, east of the A9 at 685928. The road to the farm is gated but if permission is sought, there should be no difficulty in driving through and leaving a car there. This is a most agreeable walk and we are most grateful to Wade for taking us to it. We have sampled it in rain and sunshine and never failed to enjoy it. There are always new delights with changing lights and changing seasons.

From the gate, the farm road goes straight on and joins the Wade road by the farm buildings. It passes Loch Etteridge— worth a look for water fowl if you have your binoculars with

Ruthven Barracks.

you—and Phones House, a shooting lodge. Up to this point
the road is excellently maintained. After this it can be wet in
places, but is plain to follow. It skirts a birchwood and below it
is Loch Phones, now dammed. At 716951 there was probably
a Wade bridge approached by what look like embankments

taking the road over a shallow valley. There is no sign of a bridge now but it is difficult to see what the embankments were built for if not as a run-up to a bridge. There also appear to be signs of a ford nearby but this could have been made by landrovers.

A Wade bridge in good shape is to be found at 726962. But at 739975, where the Milton Burn is wide, swift and deep there is a ford and no sign that a bridge ever existed. A tree trunk across the river at the ford makes a weir and it is a possible crossing place. If this is impracticable, desert Wade's road for a bit and use the footbridge at Luibleathann. The house can be seen on the right before you get to the burn. Take the plainly marked track which leads to it, cross the bridge and squelch your way back downstream until you reach the ford and then re-join Wade's road. The country here is very open and can be rather bleak and cold. At 742978 it is plain that there was once a bridge but the burn is not difficult to cross. The road continues for about another mile through forestry and then merges with the A9.

Two hundred yards further on, on the left hand side of the road, a gated road leads via an underpass for pedestrians only to the B970 which goes to Ruthven Barracks, one mile away. This is substantially Wade's route. The barracks occupy the top of an artificial hill which had been fortified for many centuries before they were built. It is reputed to have been one of the strongholds of the Wolf of Badenoch. The hill dominates the surrounding country and the climb up from the road is well worth it for the view alone; it is of course part of Wade's road.[9]

The next section of Wade's road will have to be imagined, preferably from the barracks. It led down to the Spey valley and to a ferry. The road would most likely have been on an embankment but all trace of it has now been washed away. The Spey meanders along a wide flat-bottomed valley and

[9] For motorists: the A9 does not go to Ruthven Barracks. To get to the barracks continue north over the Spey and take the turn off for Kingussie (A86). At the Duke of Gordon turn left and follow the road signs.

before the building of the Spey Dam flooding was more extensive than it is today. We know where the landing-place in Kingussie was, as Manse Lane was formerly Ferry Lane. The ferry was approximately where the new trunk road crosses the river.

After Kingussie the road can be traced spasmodically for some miles to the west of the old A9, now the B9152. There is a short section traceable at Lynchat, but Wade's road probably left a quarter of a mile from Manse Lane on the track leading to Kerrow, though land improvement has removed all direct trace. The drive leading to Balavil[10] (792023) gives access to the next walkable section. At the top of the drive there is a bridge over a cataract on Raitt's Burn. This is self-evidently not a Wade bridge but obviously there must have been one. To the left the road can be traced through open woodland for about half a mile. It shows all the obvious Wade signs until behind Chapel Park it swings left and becomes an estate drive. Ahead is improved farm land. From the bridge the Wade road continues north to Balavil, the house built for himself in 1790 by James MacPherson. The Wade road went straight on in front of the house and today a fence preserves the line. Follow the drive, which goes behind the house and continues as a grassy track, it then swings right and leads back to the other end of the fence and Wade's road. From here there is a mile of agreeable woodland walking with some rather attractive, sizeable conifers. This walk ends abruptly at the perimeter fence of the Kincraig Wildlife Park at 801036. The road can be seen curving away to the right and can be picked up as a grassed track running towards the park's exit gate at 809037. The Wade road then crosses the approach road to the Wild Life Park, continues for a quarter of a mile and disappears into the Meadowburn Quarry.

It continues on the far side of the quarry but this can be found most easily by starting from the next point at which

---

[10] For Balavil and also James MacPherson see page 86.
[11] Since this was written, the embankment carrying the A9 has obliterated Wade's road from the quarry to a few yards before the chapel.

Balavil House.

Wade's road coincides with the B9152 (the old A9) at 824046, a little before the small bridge over the Allt-na-Baranachd. The road can be followed uphill (back towards the quarry), above a ruined chapel[11] worth looking at in passing—and across the drive to Dunachton Lodge to the north end of the quarry. At 824046, our starting place for the walk back to the quarry, Wade's road crosses the B9152. A few yards below the bridge across the Allt-na-Baranachd there are traces of a Wade bridge. The road then continues through the birch wood to what is now the Suie Hotel. It is far from simple to trace it through the wood, although there is a section of about 200 yards in the centre that is easy to see. Although all of Wade's route is not clear, the parts that survive make the general direction clear enough. Again this is a pleasant walk, with a drink at the Suie at the end if you feel you need one.

After the hotel there is no sign of the road for one mile. The beginning of the next traceable part is again difficult to find and could easily be mistaken for a forestry path. To add to the difficulties it is not marked on the map. It is at 841069 and

Wade's road runs east. However, if it is missed, the road can be found at a later point. Opposite the drive to Alvie Lodge a track runs south to Spey Bank and a few yards along this track Wade's road crosses. To the right there is a third of a mile of easy if rather damp going through forestry, curving right to meet the B9152; this is the 'beginning' referred to above which can be difficult to find.

The left hand stretch is what could be described as a very typical Wade road, passing through forestry, much of it young, and easy pleasant going, rejoining the B9152 at 852080, about one mile on. There is no sign of a continuation immediately opposite but at 855085 there are traces of his road running roughly parallel to the B9152.

The next point where Wade's road can be traced to any extent is beyond Aviemore. At Granish (899148) it forks left and could, a few years ago, be traced as far as Avielochan, a distance of about one mile. Today, after about half a mile, Wade's road is obliterated by an embanked extension of the

A stretch of the road near Granish, Aviemore.

A95 road connecting it to the A9. His road can be traced for a short distance the other side of the embankment but is then lost under the A9. It is possible, however, to continue walking, still through forestry, by turning right after Wade's road disappears, joining the A95 (the old A9) at Avielochan.

It is more convenient to stay on the A95 for the next section, one of the longer walkable ones, of Wade's road. It is two miles north of Avielochan and to reach it turn left just opposite

A shapely Scots Pine beside the road near Kinveachy.

the point where the A95 for Grantown turns right. Go under the railway and up the sinuous ramp leading to the A9. Cross straight over the road and take the track opposite marked 'Private Road'. After 20 yards, turn right: this is Wade's road, it goes uphill, past a house with kennels adjoining. When the road forks, take the left fork—the grassed track, not the tarred one. The road continues uphill and provided care is taken to check from the map which is Wade's road and which are farm tracks, it is easy to follow. Towards the summit, there are several unusually shaped pines beside the road; they appear to be Scots Pines but they have developed the rounded outline of broad-leaved trees. When we first walked this section it was mid-October and there was the continuous roaring of stags in rut from the hills away to our left. There is no sound quite like it.

Soon after the beginning of the descent, there is a burn to be forded. There is no trace of a bridge; perhaps the burn is fuller now than in Wade's time as the land is better drained. This section of the road is maintained by the Forestry Commission and is easy going until it is crossed by the minor road leading to Carrbridge. Wade's road continues downhill to Sluggan, now sadly uninhabited. The bridge over the Dulnain is a replacement of Wade's bridge but is very similar in style. It is little used today and is grassed over. At the far side of the bridge the road is not much more than a footpath and goes straight on at a right angle to the river for about 300 yards before turning left into the birchwood. As part of it runs through peat it becomes rather boggy. At the end of the wood, the road swings right and skirts the forestry as far as Insharn.

Shortly after Insharn, a Wade bridge crosses the Allt-an-Aonaich. The road then turns right through the corner of a forestry plantation (watch for roe deer here), and then follows its west edge through to the railway. Shortly before the railway, there are the remains of another Wade bridge over a very small burn. The bridge is no longer in use, as it is very decrepit. After the railway, the path turns left and follows the line down to the A9 at Slochd Mor.

The whole walk taken at a leisurely pace took us four hours; this included time spent looking for the path after the River

At the Slochd four lines of communication converge. From the top are the railway, Wade's road, the old and the new A9.

Dulnain at Sluggan. If there is no driver to meet you, it might be more convenient to start in the middle at the point where the Wade road crosses the road from Carrbridge (875214). From here the walk south to Kinveachy and the Grantown road took us one and a half hours and the one north to Slochd two and a half hours.

A quarter of a mile north along the A9 is Slochd Summit; British Rail provides a convenient notice to mark the spot. Just after the railway line emerges from a remarkable vertical-sided cutting, on the east side of the road, opposite the summit notice, there is a steep bank and a gate in the fence. This is the beginning of the next section of Wade's road. At the start it can only be recognised as an indistinct shape in the heather but it is

The Slochd, much altered due to road reconstruction.

easier to follow than it perhaps sounds. Even where the surface cannot be seen through the heather, the hard stone core can often be felt. The ground is sometimes wet and the heather thick and tall, but in the pursuit of Wade's roads these are but small worries. The going improves for short stretches and the road is roughly gravelled where hill tracks coincide with it. It is easy to distinguish these tracks from Wade's road as they are better defined and obviously more used. Wade's road too runs generally in a straight line and much of it has the usual raised banks beside it. This is a great help in deciding which is which; we were never in serious doubt.

This is a good area for seeing mountain hares; in autumn when they are just beginning to put on their white coats they are sadly conspicuous in the dark heather.

After about two miles the road reaches its maximum height and at 818281, about one mile before the end of the section at Raigbeg, it goes into a cutting for about 200 yards. This is filled with thick juniper scrub, and so it is necessary to follow from the hillside. When the forestry in the neighbourhood of Raigbeg is reached, the road turns right and then follows along the edge, to disappear eventually under Raigbeg school. We wonder if the children know just how much history they are sitting on!

If you are walking this section from north to south, it is very easy to miss the left turn at 812285, a quarter of a mile along the forestry. The track so far is very plain and continues straight ahead as a farm road, thus there is a temptation to follow this rather than the Wade road, which is much less obvious.

From the school, the road crossed the Findhorn, probably by ferry and continued more or less in a straight line through the policies of Tomatin House, but there is no trace of this surviving. At 808294 the road can be found again above a small quarry, and from here it can be traced for a quarter of a mile west over the A9 to the farm at 804293 on the old A9, now an unclassified road, to Tomatin. It then continues along it until the drive to Tomatin House at 799296, where a short section can be seen beside a field wall. This goes to the A9 and disappears near the Allt-na-Frithe. We looked for traces of a crossing over the burn but found nothing.

Wade's road then follows the A9 for one mile, then forks right onto the B9154 (the old A9) until it reaches the old school at Moy. Here it turned left, but first the railway and now the A9 have obliterated all traces for the next mile or so. To get to the next walkable section, continue on for half a mile past Moy school until a left turn at 769342 goes straight under the railway, over the A9 and on through some forestry to a 'T' junction. The gravelled road to the right is the Wade road. This gravelled road soon gives way to a typical Wade road, easy to follow but a bit wet in patches and going on through heather until after a mile the forestry fence is reached. There is no bridge over the Allt-na-Slanaich and no sign of one ever having existed. This could have easily been forded as there is very little water in it.

Part of the Wade road through the forestry has been lost to the A9 but there is a forest path continuing on to link up with the Wade road again. The going is good here, on a well maintained, gravelled road. As is often the case, the Forestry

Commission has improved on Wade for their own use. At 364359 Wade's road forks left as a heather-filled break in the trees and there would be every excuse for thinking of it as a fire-break and so ignoring it. It leads to Mid-Lairgs. As an alternative to walking through the thick heather, continue along the new forestry road (not on the map) which leads to Auchbain. Then walk along the edge of the forestry to Mid Lairgs and so to the Wade road again.

From Mid Lairgs (which is now deserted), the road carried on to the B851, the Daviot to Fort Augustus road. When we last walked this, the whole area around Mid Lairgs was in the hands of the road engineers and gravel was being extracted extensively. How much of Wade's road at this point will actually survive is problematical. Shortly before the B851 there is a Wade bridge over the Mid Lairgs Burn. This is no longer in use. Fifty years ago, it was propped up underneath to prevent it from falling down. Now the supporting woodwork has sunk and there is a gap between it and the bridge, but the bridge is still intact. The crossing today is by a new bridge downstream of Wade's.

Wade crossed the Nairn at Faillie but the present bridge (one can take a car over it), is not his. Beyond the bridge, the road turns left through a gate and then follows the river for a few yards before turning right when the fenced section ends. It then runs steeply uphill and is much overgrown with gorse and broom but the line is reasonably easy to follow. For part of the road here, there are stone-built banks looking almost like walls and these are a good guide to its course.

At the top of the steep climb, Wade's road crosses the minor road to Daviot and continues through Culloden Forest. The first quarter of a mile is good forestry road but then it becomes a more typical Wade road, though still easy walking. After one and a half miles the forest ends. The road then goes through farmland, much of it pasture (beware animals here as the road is unfenced) until the suburbs of Inverness begin near Hilton. It continues along the Old Edinburgh road to Inverness Castle. Wade's road is tarred from 693418 and if you are starting from the Inverness end, it is possible to get a car as far as the burn at 696414.

The Road from Crieff to Dalnacardoch—

43½ miles

In 1730 Wade started work on his Crieff to Dalnacardoch Road. This was to connect the Highlands via Stirling with Glasgow and the West of Scotland.

When he began this road, there was already a road of sorts from Stirling to the River Earn. Crieff was then little more than a busy market or tryst where cattle, brought down from the Highlands, were sold and taken south to the Lowlands. This presumably would account for the existence of the road. Men and cattle crossed the Earn by ferry and it was not until after the Wade era that the bridge was built.

From two or three miles north of Crieff it is possible to walk most of the way to Aberfeldy along Wade's road. Later road-builders have followed his route in general, but there are more long stretches where his road is untouched than on other roads.

When it is relatively easy, as it is here, to compare the line Wade took, with that taken by later road builders, several points emerge:

1　Wade's road is almost always more direct than the later one.
2　It is usually uphill of the later one.
3　Wade seldom followed rivers closely.

With these points in mind, it is occasionally possible to discover short stretches of Wade road where they have not previously been spotted, because one learns to know where to look for them—at the bends on the new roads for example.

The changes in route in the post-Wade era came about through improvements in road-making skills and land drainage. These made it possible to ease the gradients on hills and the better drainage meant that roads could be built lower without being liable to flooding in winter.

Wade's Road from Crieff to Aberfeldy.

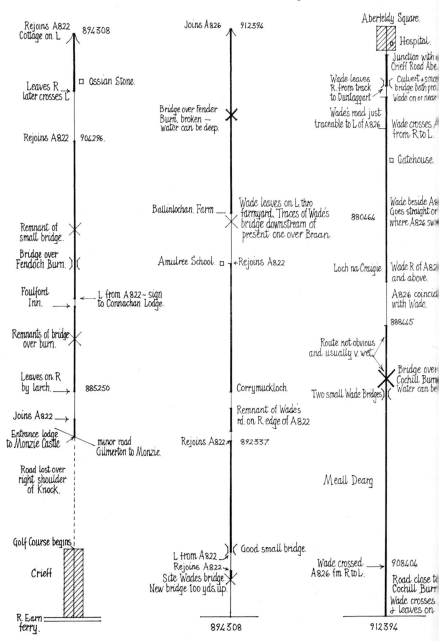

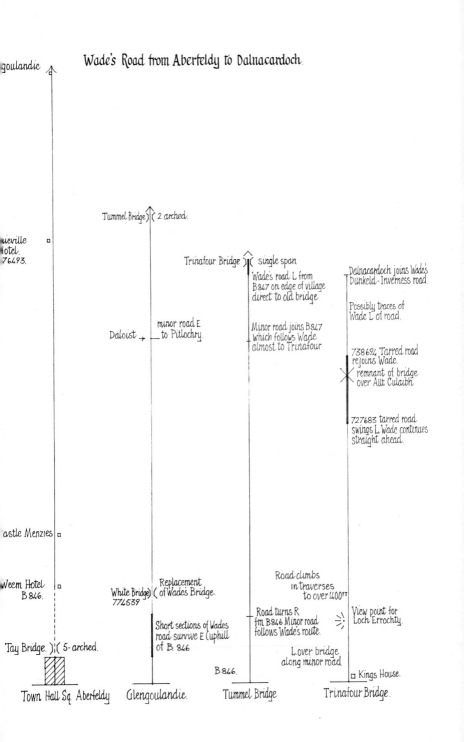

Wade's Road from Aberfeldy to Dalnacardoch.

From the river, Wade built his road in good Wade tradition, straight up hill, along what is now North Bridge Street into King Street and James Square. It is obvious that the old village of Crieff was closer to the river than the modern town and there are a number of old and architecturally interesting houses in North Bridge Street. The cobbles of King Street were put in much later, presumably to enable horses to get a grip on the steep gradient.

The line of Wade's road continues straight across the square and up Ferntower Road, past pleasant stone-built houses with colourful gardens. The one deviation from this straight line is at the bottom of Ferntower Road where Hill Street curves into High Street and James Square, past the Drummond Arms Hotel. Presumably the road was re-routed to accommodate the present 19th-century building.

After half a mile Ferntower Road ends and a private road

Wade's road going straight on from the entrance lodge to Monzie Castle.

begins, leading through the golf course. Wade's road is then lost for about one mile, having presumably been removed during the construction of the golf course and the laying out of the grounds of Monzie Castle. It went past Ferntower House (now demolished) and over the right shoulder of the Knock. A short section beyond the golf course still survives, running north from the minor road from Gilmerton to Monzie opposite the entrance lodge to Monzie Castle. It is easily seen and runs between the two dykes and is tree lined. It finishes up at the A822.

After less than half a mile, the road goes into a cutting and Wade's road leaves on the right at this point but steep banks make access impossible. There is a convenient gate shortly before the cutting. Through the gate, walk uphill along the road fence until a sizeable larch is reached. This is almost on Wade's road, which can be seen running to the right and slightly up hill, then turning left. This section is not shown on the Ordnance Survey map. It is easy going, although part of the road is covered with tussocky grass and in wet weather can be very soft.

After about one mile, a stone wall with netting on the top crosses the road. To the left there is a gate. The road goes on, dropping to a small burn once crossed by a Wade bridge, the stone retaining walls, ending neatly at ground level can be seen on both banks. The actual bridge would probably have been of wood as there is nothing to suggest the abutments of a stone arch. If this small burn had not been bridged, Wade would have had the problem of taking the road down to water level and bringing it up again, as the burn runs several feet below the level of the surrounding land.

From there on the road can, with care, be traced across fields to a much improved meadow adjoining the Foulford Inn. Beyond the gate is a small ridge which still shows the unmistakable 'nick' indicating quite clearly where the road was. There is no trace of the short section of the road from there to the A822.

Fifty yards north from the Foulford Inn (signposted to Connachan Lodge), Wade's road turns left and rejoins the A822 about two miles further on in the Sma' Glen. This is a very pleasant and easy walk. After 200 yards, it crosses a small tributory of the Fendoch Burn. Here there was once a Wade bridge of two or three small arches. This is surprising considering the size of the burn. There is now a typical County Council culvert with the burn flowing through pipes. The stones above and around the pipes are most probably the ones Wade used. Further on there is a much reconstructed Wade bridge over the Fendoch Burn itself.

The road follows round the edge of the forestry for a few yards then turns right to go up hill through a field. (The Wade road at this point is far less plain than the section just walked. Look for two sleeper bridges over the ditches, leading to a double gate. Through the gate, Wade's road can be seen slightly to the right.) It winds as it climbs and at a 'T' junction meets a well-defined farm track where it turns right. At the 'T' junction is a burn, where the remains of Wade's crossing can be seen.

The Ossian Stone.

The road winds its way gently through grassland and is very easy walking. The grass gives way to heather as the descent to the Sma' Glen begins. Wade's road-making problems are brought home to us by the sizeable loop that he is obliged to make to avoid an impossibly steep descent to a small unnamed burn at 904291, with another almost equally steep climb on the other side. The whole road is very plain to see, the last part running almost parallel to the main road.

Wade's road and the A822 coincide for another half mile. The next two sections of road are short and never more than a few yards from the modern road. The first section is east of the road and runs through fields from 897301 to 896305. At the north end is the Ossian Stone, a large boulder seven feet high and six feet square. The other short section can be seen across the road, beginning almost opposite to where this one ends.

The process by which the Ossian Stone or, Clach Ossian in its Gaelic form came to be so named is of some interest. The boulder is first referred to by Burt writing from first-hand knowledge in 1736 or thereabouts:

> I have so lately mentioned Glen Almond, in the road from Crief, northwards, that I cannot forebear a digression, though at my first setting out, in relation to a piece of antiquity that happened to be discovered in that vale not many hours before I passed through it in one of my journeys southwards.
>
> A small part of the way through this glen having been marked out by two rows of camp-colours, placed at a good distance one from another, whereby to describe the intended breadth and regularity of the road by the eye, there happened to lie directly in the way an exceedingly large stone, and, as it had been made a rule from the beginning, to carry on the roads in straight lines, as far as the way would permit, not only to give them a better air, but to shorten the passenger's journey, it was resolved that the stone should be removed, if possible, though otherwise the work might have been carried along on either side of it.

The soldiers, by vast labour, with their levers and jacks or hand-screws, tumbled it over and over until they got it quite out of the way, although it was of such an enormous size that it might be a matter of great wonder how it could ever be removed by human strength and art, especially to such who had never seen an operation of that kind: and, upon their digging a little way into that part of the ground where the centre of the base had stood, there was found a small cavity about two feet square, which was guarded from the outside earth at the bottom, top and side, by square flat stones.

This hollow contained some ashes, scraps of bones, and half burnt ends of stalks of heath: which last we concluded to be a small remnant of a funeral pile. Upon the whole, I think there is no room to doubt but it was the urn of some considerable Roman officer, and the best of the kind that could be provided in their military circumstances; and that it was so seems plainly to appear from its vicinity to the Roman camp, the engines that must have been employed to remove that vast piece of rock, and the unlikeliness that it should, or could, have ever been done by the natives of the country. But certainly the design was to preserve those remains from the injuries of rains or melting snows, and to prevent their being profaned by the sacrilegious hands of those they called barbarians, for that reproachful name, you know, they gave to the people of almost all nations but their own.

As I returned the same way from the Lowlands I found the Officer, with his party of working soldiers, not far from the stone, and asked him what was become of the urn?

To this he answered, that he had intended to preserve it in the condition I left it, till the Commander-in-Chief had seen it, as a curiosity, but that it was not in his power to do so; for soon after the discovery was known to the Highlanders, they assembled from distant parts, and having formed themselves into a body, they carefully gathered up the relics, and marched with them, in solemn procession, to a new place of burial, and there discharged their fire-arms[12] over the grave, as supposing the deceased had been a military officer.

You will believe that the recital of all this ceremony led me to ask the reason of such homage to the ashes of a person supposed to have been dead almost two thousand years. I did so; and the officer, who was himself a native of the hills, told me that they (the Highlanders) firmly believed that if a dead body should be known to lie above ground, or be disinterred by malice, or the accidents of torrents of water, &c and care was not taken to perform to it the proper rites, then there would arise such storms and tempests as would destroy their corn, blow away their huts, and all sorts of other misfortunes would follow till that duty was performed and you may here recollect what I told you so long ago, of the great regard the Highlanders have for the remains of their dead; but this notion is entirely Roman.

Plainly the Highlanders' action was inspired by the ancient and widely held belief that the dead cannot lie unburied without retribution falling on those who have allowed it to happen. Burt's informant was a Highland (and therefore Gaelic speaking) officer and it is quite incredible that he would not have been told if there were any tradition linking the remains with Ossian, or that he would have omitted this interesting fact from his account.

But fifty years later the remains *have* become those of Ossian, said to be an epic poet of the third century. Thomas Newte (Tour in England and Scotland) reports what he was told by people living in Glen Almond in 1785:

---

[12] It seems strange that, after the Disarming Acts of 1715 and 1725, the soldiers should have ignored what appears to be the Highlanders' illegal possession of fire-arms. However, licences to keep and carry arms were given to trustworthy 'Foresters, Drovers and dealers in Cattle' who belonged to clans which had surrendered their arms. Wade issued over 200 of these licences in 1725 alone. Burt does not suggest that *all* the Highlanders re-burying the remains had guns. It could well have been a token volley fired-off by the members of the party who had these licences.

The people of the country, for several miles around, to the number of three or four score of men, venerating the memory of the Bard, rose with one consent, and carried away the bones, with bag pipes playing, and other funeral rites, and deposited them with much solemnity within a large circle of stones, on the lofty summit of a rock, sequestered and of difficult access, where they might never more be disturbed by mortal feet or hands, in the wild recesses of western Glen Almond.

This linking of the remains with Ossian is a consequence of the work of James Macpherson (1736–96). He claimed to have found manuscripts of parts of Gaelic poems by Ossian which he published in 'translation' in 1760. Two or three years later he published a 'translation' of the complete epic of Fingal that he said he had discovered. The poems had an enormous success in Scotland, in spite of Samuel Johnson's sceptical demand to see the supposed manuscripts.

It is now generally accepted that Johnson's scepticism was justified; there were no manuscripts to produce, the poems were Macpherson's own work. But to admit this is not to deny their literary value, which some scholars at least, think to be substantial. What is quite certain is that Macpherson's poems had so seized the Scottish imagination in his own life-time that they generated a 'folk-history' to accompany them, as here in Glen Almond where a chance discovery of the interred ashes of a completely unknown man is said, half a century later, to be the discovery of the grave of Ossian.

Macpherson was rich enough towards the end of his life to have a handsome house built for himself by Robert Adam. It still stands; it is at Lynchat a little north of Kingussie on Wade's road from Dunkeld to Inverness. He called it Belleville although today the traditional form of the name, Balavil, has been re-adopted (see page 68).

Wade's road continues as the A822 to Newton Bridge. It is usually thought that Wade's bridge over the Almond was on the site of the present one and it is said that traces of it can be seen underneath, but we failed to see any. However, immediately north of the bridge, through a gate on the right

Wade's bridge over a burn near Newton.

hand side of the road, a section of what appears to be a Wade
road can be plainly seen, heading for the river. Shortly before
reaching it, the road changes direction and with this change of
direction its character also changes and it appears to be of later
date. It is probably a farm track. If the line of the 'Wade' road is
continued to the river bank it leads to a collection of large
moss-covered stones which could have been part of a bridge
footing. The bank both up and downstream is free from such
stones, so this would suggest that it was here that Wade
crossed the Almond and the stones are all that remain of his
bridge. There are no signs of a similar footing on the opposite
bank, but much of this has been altered to prevent the road
being undercut by the river. This section is worth a visit so that
you can indulge your own speculations.

A few yards past the bridge, the Wade road again leaves the
A822, this time on the left hand side. It immediately crosses a
very pleasant grassy bridge over a burn, loops to the right and
is clearly shown by marker stones until, after about one and a
half miles, it reaches the A822 at 892337.

It is known that Wade often made fords to cross rivers and
later bridged them. In some cases this was because the road
was ready to be used but no bridge masons were available. In
other cases he found later that bridges were necessary as fords
were washed away in winter spates. Looking back to this
bridge from the north, two roads can be seen; the better
preserved road leading in a loop to the bridge and another
road, slightly less obvious, leading straight to the burn, which
originally must have been forded. When the bridge was put in,
this road would have fallen into disuse. The loop on the later
road was necessary to avoid an impossibly sharp turn onto the
bridge.

After the bridge, the road is wet, but it gets drier and then
enters a cutting. Here it is full of stones and for the next few
yards is rather uncomfortable going. It then gets wet again as it
runs close to the A822. The last part is half under the A822 but
its marker stones survive. It ends at a gate.

Shortly after the end of this section and on the other side of
the road are a few yards of Wade road. They can be seen from
the A822 and are hardly worth walking. The next walkable

section is from Corrymuckloch to Amulree, a distance of a little over one mile. Again the improvement of grassland has meant that a short section of the road has disappeared. It now begins in a field behind Corrymuckloch and is most easily located by going to the top of the road to the farm. There is very little to the left of this road, but to the right Wade's road runs pleasantly through open moorland and is adequately supplied with marker stones. The last section runs steeply down to Amulree and today is used as a peat road and peat stacks line it.

At Amulree the A822 crosses the Braan by a post-Wade bridge. Just before the bridge on the left hand side is the Amulree Hotel. This was a King's House but has been altered out of any recognition. The Wade bridge was a few yards down stream from the present one; there are slight traces of the road on the south bank and much plainer ones on the north, with what are probably remains of Wade's bridge in the water between them. A bridge on this site would continue Wade's

North of Newton the line of the road is often unclear. It is discernible between a double rank of marker stones towards the cutting, top centre.

'peat-stack' road in a straight line to the river and then again straight on to the next section. This cuts out the loop occurring in the present road as it crosses the new bridge.

The next section leaves the A822 via the farmyard of Ballinlochan (the map marks the farm but does not name it), about 100 yards after the Amulree bridge on the left hand side. The road is at first a farm road and is easy going. Wade's bridge over the Fender Burn has fallen and as the burn is both fast and deep, crossing this can be difficult and damp. The easiest crossing place is probably some yards upstream. Once over the burn, the road goes straight up hill. It is rough, stony and obviously never used. At one point there is a fence across it without a gate. At 908385 it makes a sharp turn right, and a well-used farm road (which the map does not show), comes in on the left and joins Wade's road.

The road then continues along a wall and swings left crossing a small fenced area, between the wall and some forestry. To the left of Wade's road there is a gate; using this saves climbing two fences. At the north-west corner of this forestry, Wade's road swings half left. This has to be remembered, as his road is much less defined than the farm track which swings right and goes downhill. The temptation is to follow this.

A short distance after the left turn, a corner of a block of conifers, not shown on the map, encroaches on Wade's road. Continue along the edge of the conifers, through the gate at the corner and after a few yards Wade's road can be seen emerging from the trees. From here, it is plain and runs straight down to reach the A826 at 912395. It leaves directly at the opposite side of the road. This is a plain, typical Wade road, easily walked through heather for three-quarters of a mile and runs close to the Cochill Burn. It then re-crosses the A826 at 908404.

The next three miles of Wade's road includes the wettest stretch we have encountered. The road begins as a plain track through heather, part of which is used as a farm road and has been re-surfaced. Several burns draining down from Meall Dearg make the going wet in places, but otherwise walking this part is quite easy. There are raised banks at the sides of the road and as it climbs there are occasional marker stones to show the way. One mile after the summit, there are two small Wade bridges in a line and very close together. The first one is over a burn, the second is almost dry. A few yards further on there is the larger Cochill Burn. There is no sign of a bridge over this, but there are a number of boulders on the bank which could once have been part of a bridge. As the Cochill Burn is wide and swiftly flowing in the winter, a bridge could have been washed away, as many other Wade bridges were. However, in Wellingtons it is still possible to cross the burn, dry foot.

The next third of a mile is the very wet section. The road was built on an embankment, the only possible way Wade had of getting across this swampy valley. It went in a straight line, making for higher, firmer ground. Today it is anything but easy walking. The embankment has disintegrated in a number of places, it is overgrown with very thick heather and is full of holes nourising underground water courses. A burn flowing out of Loch-na-Craige to join the Cochill Burn runs along the left side of the road and at one point another burn runs neatly along the other side, then crosses it to join the Loch-na-Craige Burn. As the road begins to climb, the embankment ends. It then enters a heather-filled cutting and walking along this can be rather tiring. It takes quite an abrupt turn and climbs to join the A826 at 887445.[13]

A piece of general advice. If the going gets too wet and the road defeats you, it is well to remember that a turn right and uphill will bring you over rough heather to the 'safety' of the A826. It is perhaps easier to walk this section from North to South. The first part of the road (to the end of the heather-filled cutting) is never in doubt. When it turns left, the road is completely straight for well over one mile and can be seen ahead descending Meall Dearg. If it is not too misty, this can give a mark to aim for. This section of Wade road is unique in one particular. The later replacement road (A826) is well uphill of Wade's. The reverse is normally true.

---

[13] Since we last walked this section much of the area has been forested. Fortunately Wade's road has been left intact.

A few yards beyond the south end of Loch-na-Craige Wade's road is to be found to the east of the A826. Loch-na-Craige is a beautiful loch edged with hills and Wade's road is never far from it. It is a pleasant track through heather and after three-quarters of a mile the A826 curves to join it. The two roads then coincide for a short distance. At the mile stone, the A826 turns left and Wade's road continues straight on, again through heather, until it disappears in cultivated grassland surrounding Gate House, once thought to be an Inn but now a keeper's house. The road ran roughly parallel to the present one, past the house and into birchwood where it can once again be seen and followed until it crosses the present road obliquely at 785480, about one mile from Gate House. The short section on the west side of the A862 is not very obvious. It runs between two small hills then rejoins the road at 873483 and shortly after leaves it again on the right hand side. This is the last time the two roads cross before Aberfeldy.

This last part of the road can be picked up from the left hand side of the farm road leading to Duntaggart at 868485. To begin with it runs briefly along the track to Borlick but where that swings right, Wade's road goes straight on. Just where his road leaves the Borlick track there is a bridge of stone slabs which is probably Wade's. There is certainly a Wade bridge at 867486. At the time when we walked this road, the stones that Wade's soldiers so carefully positioned for marker and boundary stones, were being equally carefully removed by a farmer's workers to increase the farm's useable acreage. By such means is our landscape altered to meet our needs. Just before the road reaches Aberfeldy Hospital, it disappears under improved grassland, but the line has been preserved and the road leading from the hospital to the centre of the town is still called the Old Crieff Road. It is now a cul-de-sac. From the hospital it is a short distance to the River Tay and the Aberfeldy bridge.

Aberfeldy is a fairly prosperous little town, well worth stopping in. The river and its immediate surrounds give an impression of ease and space. Near the bridge is the memorial to the Black Watch. It would be a pity just to pass over the bridge without feeling something of its glories. Unlike Wade's bridges at Tummel and Trinafour, the Aberfeldy bridge is still in full use. It is not wide enough to carry two-way traffic and the rise to the centre arch makes it impossible to see from one end to the other, so traffic is controlled by lights at each end. This bridge is the only ashlar bridge Wade built. Ashlars are cut and dressed blocks of stone which fit together with the minimum of mortar. Every other Wade bridge, even Highbridge, was a rubble bridge, where natural pieces of stone are fitted together as well as possible and the gaps then filled in with copious supplies of mortar.

Presumably the Tay bridge had to be built of ashlars as it was not only the longest bridge he built (it is nearly 400 feet long) but also the one involving the widest span—the centre arch of its five is 60 feet across. An ashlar bridge is much stronger, as well as more graceful, than a rubble one. The architect was William Adam and Wade gathered together the most skilled team of bridge masons that he could find, bringing them not only from Edinburgh and lowland Scotland, but also from northern England, a region whose bridge-masons were particularly famed at that time. Stockpiling of materials began in 1732, construction in April 1733. By the autumn the bridge was in use, though the

The bridge at Aberfeldy.

parapets remained to be built in the following year. This is amazingly rapid progress. The pride Wade rightly felt in his handiwork can be seen from the plaques recording its building which he set upon it and the four graceful obelisks with which he ornamented it. Wade is probably more remembered for this bridge than for anything else he did; it is exactly the memorial he would have wanted.

Over the bridge, the houses give way to fields and almost immediately the road swung left, across what is now farmland to Wade's local headquarters, which today, much altered and enlarged, survives as the Weem Hotel. There is a portrait of Wade outside; apparently he was fond of having himself painted, and his stay there is recorded. After Weem Wade took his road along the Tay valley at the foot of the hills, up the valley of the Keltney Burn and on to Tummel Bridge. The hotel at Coshieville is supposed to have housed troops working on this stretch of road. This route north is still the one used today by the B846—a tribute to the surveying and

The older part of Weem Hotel used by Wade as his headquarters.

planning of Wade and his team. The only certain traces of the original road are a few short sections to the east of the B846 between Glengoulandie and White Bridge.

Wade bridged the River Tummel, where there was a King's House, and his bridge stands today, although it is closed to all traffic except pedestrians. The B846 goes over a nondescript iron bridge beside it. Wade's bridge is of pleasing line, with two rounded arches. The river is not very wide here and normally the smaller northern arch is dry. It was put in to give the bridge additional waterway to cope with spates; there are other Wade bridges with these 'spate arches'. It took bridge engineers many years to grasp fully the extent of the problem that winter spates gave them. Some of the earlier Wade bridges had been washed away at this season and Telford in the early nineteenth century was still making the same mistake and losing bridges which were too small, much to his cost and inconvenience.

A mile or so after the bridge, Wade's road turns right, leaving the B846 and the Tummel valley, and climbs to over 1000 feet before dropping steeply to Glen Errochty and Trinafour. The present road crosses the Errochty Water downstream of Wade's bridge. To get to it, cross the new one, turn left immediately and another 200 yards will bring you to it. It is now grassed over and like Tummel bridge it is closed to all traffic but pedestrians. Cross the bridge (it leads to a church) and continue along the road until you reach the one you have just left, this was Wade's route. Trinafour bridge is a very difficult one to view, rather like Highbridge, as it too is in a deep, steep-sided valley. Wade obviously thought this the best crossing place. The climb out of Glen Errochty is so steep that the road has to be traversed. There are fine views of the Loch Errochty dam from some way up the traverses.

After crossing a small burn flowing out of Dubh Lochan today's road turns left to avoid a steep gradient, but Wade's road, true to form, continues straight on. It leaves at 727683 just after a milestone on the east side of the road. The first few yards of Wade's road were lost when earth was moved to reinforce the embankment of the present road, but there is no difficulty in seeing it from the embankment. The road goes down through the heather to the Ault Culaibh. Parts of the Wade bridge can be seen at 728690. The burn is not very wide and can easily be crossed dry foot. Wade's road continues and joins the present road at 727693. From here it is more or less on the present road until it joins the A9 at Dalnacardoch.

The Road from Dalwhinnie to Fort Augustus—28 miles

This road was made in 1731 and with its completion, Wade's network of roads was finished. It provided a much shorter route from the south to Fort Augustus and the west coast than the existing one via Inverness.

Unfortunately, the best direct route involved going over the Corrieyairack Pass at a height of over 2500 feet and in deciding to use this route Wade made the only major planning error in his whole time as Commander-in-Chief. He appears to have been undeterred by the height of the summit and to have seen the road as a challenge to his road-making skills. What he did not fully appreciate was the severity of the Highland winter. Heavy falls of snow, drifting in the strong winds, blocked the pass for many months each winter and long stretches of the road were damaged when the snows melted.

Wade's Corrieyairack road presented problems rather than solved them, but connecting Fort Augustus to the south seems always to have been fraught with difficulties. Early in the nineteenth-century, it was eventually decided, as part of Telford's road-building programme, to adopt the longer route which is still substantially in use, linking the Great Glen road, in the neighbourhood of the south end of Loch Lochy, with a new road running up Glen Spean. This new road, now the A86 for most of its length, was to run from the new Spean Bridge to Kingussie to join the Dunkeld to Inverness road.

The route was first surveyed in 1805 but there were many delays and it was 1818 before the road was finished.

When his new road was completed the Corrieyairack section of Wade's road dropped out of use, except as a drove road. The section between Dalwhinnie and Drumgask, however, was maintained as a link between Telford's road and the south. Pylons now follow the line of the pass and we are mainly indebted to the Hydro-Electric Board for such recent maintenance as the road has received.

Dalwhinnie – Fort Augustus Road   Sheet 1

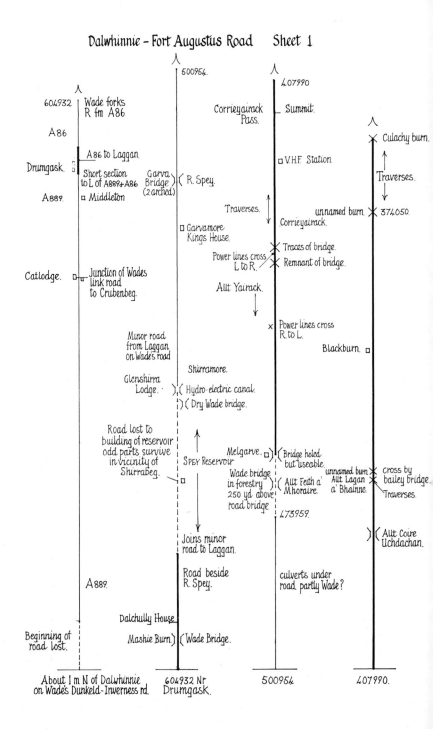

604932 — Wade forks R fm A86

A86

Drumgask.

A86 to Laggan.

Short section to L of A889 & A86

A889. □ Middleton

Garva Bridge (2 arched))(R. Spey.

Catlodge. □ Junction of Wades link road to Crubenbeg.

Minor road from Laggan on Wade's road

Glenshirra Lodge. ·)(Hydro-electric canal.
)(Dry Wade bridge.

Shirramore.

Road lost to building of reservoir odd parts survive in vicinity of Shirrabeg.

Spey Reservoir

Joins minor road to Laggan.

A889.

Road beside R. Spey.

Dalchuilly House

Mashie Burn)(Wade Bridge.

Beginning of road lost.

About 1 m N of Dalwhinnie on Wade's Dunkeld-Inverness rd.

604932 Nr Drumgask.

500954.

Corrieyairack Pass.

□ V.H.F. Station.

Traverses.

□ Garvamore Kings House.

Traces of bridge.
Power lines cross L to R. Remnant of bridge.

Allt Yairack.

Power lines cross R. to L.

Melgarve. □)(Bridge holed but useable.

Wade bridge in forestry 250 yd above road bridge)(Allt Feith a' Mhoraire.

473959.

culverts under road. partly Wade?

500954

407990.

Summit.

Corrieyairack.

unnamed burn. ✕ 374050.

Blackburn. □

unnamed burn ✕ Allt Lagan a' Bhainne.

)(Allt Coire Uchdachan.

Culachy burn.

Traverses.

cross by bailey bridge.

Traverses.

407990.

The Upper Spey in spate

The road starts from Wade's Dunkeld to Inverness road just north of Dalwhinnie. It coincides with the A889 to Drumgask, passing through Catlodge where it makes a left turn. At Drumgask, where the A889 descends steeply to join the A86 (Fort William to Newtonmore road) Wade's road leaves just as the descent begins, runs above and a short way to the left of it, in front of the Drumgask cottages, and descends to join the A86 a few yards further on. For once the gradient on Wade's road is easier than that on the present one.

Half a mile west of Drumgask, at 605936, Wade's road forks right from the A86 as a heathery track and shortly after joins the drive to Dalchully House where there is still a good Wade bridge over the Mashie Burn. When the drive turns sharp left, Wade's road continues beside the Spey and joins the present minor road from Laggan to Garva Bridge, continues on it for a quarter of a mile and then makes for the reservoir where it is lost for half a mile or so. It can be traced in the neighbourhood of Sherrabeg and intermittently for a further half mile.

The next remnant of the road is the dry bridge at 555932, just before the present road crosses the canal. It is probable, from the angle of the bridge that Wade's road was on the left hand side of the present road for this last part. After the canal bridge we are back on his road once more.

How the bridge came to be dry is of some interest. In 1946 the dam on the Spey was built with the purpose of forming a reservoir with the same water level as Loch Crunachdan and a canal was constructed joining them. Both lochs ultimately help power British Aluminium's hydro-electric generators at Fort William and the water from them now leaves by a tunnel at the south end of Loch Crunachdan. Before the building of the dam, there was a burn flowing from Loch Crunachdan into the Spey; this has now ceased to exist. It was this burn that the Wade bridge crossed. From the far side of the canal, the Wade road is much improved. It goes through Garvamore where there was a King's House which has been neglected for years, but now happily is being restored. Garvamore was also one of the 'stances' when the road over the Corrieyairack became a drove road. A 'stance' was an area where drovers regularly over-nighted their cattle, a place with grazing and water. Melgarve was another such stance. Ideally they occurred at ten- to twelve-mile intervals the distance cattle could cover in a day without losing condition.

A mile on is Garva Bridge, a very fine two-arched bridge over the Spey and incidentally the first two-arched bridge that Wade built. The arches are unusually widely separated, as the centre column is built on a rock jutting out of the bed of the Spey. It almost gives the impression of two single-arched bridges joined in succession. The narrow bridge and the rather high parapets give it a closed-in feeling. After the bridge the tarred road is maintained by the Hydro-Electric Board and has suffered a great deal of subsidence but it is still possible to drive the four miles on to the Allt Feith-a-Mhoraire just before Melgarve. Two of the culverts on this stretch show signs of being originally Wade's although there is new work on top.

The wooden bridge across the Allt Feith-a-Mhoraire and some of the road each side of it are not Wade's. Two hundred yards upstream of the wooden bridge, Wade's bridge, in surprisingly good shape, survives. It is in a block of forestry but can be seen from the road. We could find no sign of the approach road. It probably left the present road at about the

point where the forestry begins (477958) and re-joined it at
Melgarve, going behind the small hillock west of the forestry.
This makes a straighter line than the present road.

In Wade's time most of the Corrieyairack burns were
bridged. All the bridges survive in part or entirely, but where
they are not useable, crossing is not difficult. While crossing
one swiftly flowing burn on our last walk, a small trout swam
onto one of our boots. To have caught it would at that
moment have been a crime. A great deal of over-dramatised
writing exists about the difficulties of the Corrieyairack but it
should not be taken too seriously. You do need a good day,
but on the other hand we met a party of walkers who were
spending two days in the area and they had had no difficulty in
finding the path in mist. It depends on your stamina and ability
to walk twelve miles over rough country. But walking it in
one stretch does, of course, involve having a car at the other
end.

Garva bridge across the Spey.

There are four or five miles of rough but delightful walking from Melgarve to the summit which is over 2500 feet. The Corrie Yairack from which the pass gets its name is the corrie on the right hand side of the road just below the traverses. The burn flowing out of it and accompanying Wade's road almost back to Melgarve is the Allt Yairack. The most spectacular part of the walk is the climb up the thirteen traverses, zig-zags or hairpins as they are commonly called, close to the summit.

Looking east from a point above Allt a' Mhill Ghairbh near Melgarve.

Take heart for this is the most tiring part of the entire walk. Wade built eighteen traverses, a considerable engineering feat, as each one had to be supported by stone retaining walls; however, five of the traverses were taken out in a later reconstruction. There is a small VHF station half a mile from the summit.

Throughout this walk the route is never in question, although the weather often is. The summit is rather exposed but we found it most exhilarating. Its exposure is compensated for by the marvellous view. Even on a dull day it is not without appeal. We once lunched at the top of the pass in late October sunshine and felt almost over warm. There is quite a lot of birdlife to be seen and heard and on occasion ptarmigan are present.

The road first drops gently down and then gets steeper. Two miles after the summit there is a pleasant, single-arched Wade bridge over the Allt-Coire Uchdachan. The bridge is intact, but is bypassed by a new one. Half a mile on, the road descends in traverses to the Allt Lagan-a-Bhainne. Straight ahead from the point where a new section of road swings sharply right to descend to a Bailey bridge put in by the R.E.s in 1961, are the remains of a Wade bridge over the burn. Until recently there was a suspension bridge above it, but this too has gone, though its concrete anchorages are very obvious.

Over the Allt Lagan-a-Bhainne, Wade took his road uphill. It swung right and crossed a small unnamed burn in a deep ravine. This bridge too has fallen, but the footings and the retaining walls for the road survive. In his usual way, Wade kept his road uphill even though it meant building an extra bridge. The present road is lower, and descends to the level of the Allt Lagan-a-Bhainne and crosses it by the Bailey bridge at a point below the confluence of the two burns that Wade bridged. After the second of his broken bridges, Wade's road can be seen plainly running downhill and the road from the Bailey bridge joins it. This new road and the Bailey bridge are not on the map.

It was just about here, at a sheltered point between the hills, nicknamed 'Snugborough' by Wade's soldiers, that he gave them an Oxfeast. The date was 30 October, the King's

The Corrieyairack Pass, hairpin bends marked in to show the course of the road.

birthday and we are told that six oxen were roasted. This was to celebrate the completion of the road in 1732, although the bulk of the work was done in 1731.

After 'Snugborough' the road climbs and then makes its way gently down Glentarff, then goes steeply down in traverses to the Culachy Burn. Just before the traverses begin at 374050, there are remains of a bridge, probably Wade's. There is another bridge, heavily repaired with timber, over the Culachy Burn at 368053. The road continues beside the grounds of Culachy House, crosses a minor road and finishes on another of Wade's roads, that from Fort Augustus to Fort William, now the A82. The last part of the Corrieyairack road as it descends to the minor road, has a gradient steeper than one in ten—it drops 500 feet in less than one mile.

As we have said above, there is a great deal of over-dramatic writing about the horrors and terrors of crossing the Corrieyairack Pass. In contrast Wade himself said, 'The new road . . . is now made as easy and practicable for wheeled carriages as any road in the country.' But it must be admitted that in snow the road could be a killer. Those who died of exposure were almost invariably pedestrians. Fort Augustus is less than 100 feet above sea level and even Melgarve is over 1500 feet below the summit. In winter, weather at these levels is very little indication of conditions on the tops and by the time travellers were certain they had misjudged their chances, they were probably too weary to get back.

A final practical note. If you are walking this road in two stages, at the Fort Augustus end start at the point where it leaves the minor road (373072). There is even a notice to tell you that you are on Wade's Corrieyairack road. Snugborough is just about half way and fortunately too, both halves are about equally strenuous. Perhaps we have been fortunate, but we have always walked it without too much difficulty. But then we have always known there was a hot bath and copious food and drink at the end, a very encouraging thought.

The Link Road

It is known that Wade built a link road between his Dunkeld to Inverness road and his Dalwhinnie to Fort Augustus road. Its purpose was to provide a quick route between the barracks at Ruthven and Forts Augustus and William, avoiding the long detour south by Dalwhinnie or the even longer one north by Inverness. The link road ran between Crubenbeg Bridge where the Inverness road crossed the Truim and Catlodge where the Fort Augustus road changed direction, going west instead of north. It was probably built in 1732.

In 1746 Ruthven Barracks were captured by the Jacobites and burnt, leaving only the stout stone walls standing. The barracks were never rebuilt and so the link road was no longer needed. In this sort of country it does not take long for unmaintained roads to become overgrown and today there are very few traces of Wade's road remaining. We know, however, that it went through 'Coraldie'. 'Coraldie' existed as recently as half a century ago. It lay on the minor road between Catlodge and the A9, but all that remains now are foundations of a few buildings on the north side of the road at 665935. So from this point at least, the line of Wade's link road is preserved by the minor road to Catlodge. The problem is how it got here from Crubenbeg Bridge.

The first part from the bridge is clear; the road runs past the old school, now a farmhouse, through a gate, uphill and past a burnt-out house. There is a notice in front of the school saying there is a right of way to Laggan. The house has in fact been burnt out twice. The first fire was in 1866 and in the field below the road are the graves of Charlotte and Jane Macpherson who died in this fire. It is carefully recorded on the gravestone that the ground had been consecrated, to scotch any suggestion of suicides being buried in unconsecrated ground. The second fire occurred almost a century later, in 1967. This time there has been no rebuilding.

Dalwhinnie – Fort Augustus Road
Sheet 2.

Link Road

A889 ——— Catlodge (Dalwhinnie – Fort Augustus Road.)

Breakachy ▫ —

Fort Augustus 1½ mls

A82. —

▫ | Minor road linking A82 & A862

— Culachy House.

665935. | Coraldie

Descent thro' heather.

Crubenbeg Crags. | road traceable for short lengths.

Crubenbeg (burnt out.) ▫

Former School. ▫

Culachy Burn.

Crubenbeg Bridge. (Dunkeld – Inverness Rd.)

After the house, the road swings left, still climbing, crosses a grass field where there are traces of what may be Wade's work and goes through a gate in a wall. Near the gate, another notice points the way back to the Perth road. From here onward there are no certain signs of Wade's road and there has always been some question as to its route. There are two possibilities. Wade may have taken his road right, that is, along the track parallel to the wall, continuing on what is now a forestry path, to come out on today's minor road to Catlodge at 678943. The difficulty in crediting this as Wade's route is that it is not the most direct, which is very un-Wade like. The alternative route is the one we favour.

From the gate, this route goes uphill, at right angles to the wall, through the birch scrub and over the right shoulder of Crubenbeg, just below the crags and then swings left to drop down to Coraldie. There are signs of a track through the birch scrub and below the crags, and also in the neighbourhood of Coraldie itself, that is all. But like Coraldie the track was marked on maps of fifty years ago; it survived as long as Coraldie did.

This route is much more typical of Wade in its directness and disregard of steepish climbs than the other possibility. We have walked it without undue difficulty.

Highland Forts—
An Historical Summary

There were four forts in the Highlands which Wade connected by his roads.

1 Inverness There had been forts in the city from the twelfth century, but not all on the same site. Wade's fort was on the same site as the present Castle. When he arrived in Scotland little remained of the previous fort so a new one was started in 1726. He called it Fort George after the King. It must not be confused with the present Fort George at Ardersier Point some miles to the east of the city. This was not built until 1756. Wade's Fort George survived until 1746 when it was captured in the rebellion and demolished.

2 Fort Augustus In 1716 there was a small fort here and there may have been one earlier. Wade thought it too far from Loch Ness and began a new one in 1727. He called it Fort Augustus though for a time the village around it was known as Wadesborough. This fort, like Fort George was captured in 1746 and largely destroyed. The first fort was known as Killichuimen.

3 Fort William There had been a fort in this area since 1650. It was strengthened by successive military commanders including Wade and unlike the other two, successfully withstood a siege in 1746. It had several names before the present one, of these Inverlochy and Maryborough are the best known.

4 Ruthven This mound has had forts and castles on it from the fourteenth century. It is sixty feet high and is probably an artificial hillock. The present barracks were started in 1717 and extended by Wade in 1734. Ruthven too was captured in 1746 and burnt. Whereas little or nothing of the other three forts remain today, the walls of Ruthven stand almost entire, a conspicuous landmark in the Spey Valley.

There was also a fifth fort but it was badly sited and never of much importance. Wade never considered linking it by road to the others. It was at Bernera in Glen Elg on what is now the Road to the Isles. It was a copy of the first phase of Ruthven. In 1786 Knox found that its garrison consisted of 'an aged corporal and his equally aged wife'.

Epilogue

Today, tracing Wade's roads is an antiquarian study carried out in surroundings which vary from the agreeable to the superb. To the excitement of discovery is added the bonus of identifying the plants and wildlife of the Highlands and the elemental pleasure of walking the hills. But the roads were political in origin and nothing short of revolutionary in their effects. They more than anything else ended the geographical isolation of the Highlands, and this being ended, changes came fast. Not everyone approved of these changes and we shall end by presenting some varied view-points from the eighteenth century.

The government was quite clear in its objectives and when Wade was sent to Scotland in 1724 his brief included the instruction 'to suggest to the King such other remedies as may conduce to the quiet of His Majesty's faithful subjects, and the good settlement of that part of the Kingdom.' That he saw in his task in the same light is clear from his 1728 report. Talking of the projected road from Inverness to Perth, Wade points out that it 'will open a short and speedy communication with the troops quartered in the low country, contribute to civilise the Highlanders, and in my humble opinion will prove the most effectual means to continue them in a due obedience to your Majesty's Government.'

Edward Burt knew the Highlands as well as any Highlander, since he lived and worked there for decades. About 1736 he reports sympathetically to an English friend on 'The Objections made to these new Roads and Bridges':

> Those Chiefs and other gentlemen complain, that thereby an easy passage is opened into their country for strangers, who, in time by their suggestions of liberty, will destroy or weaken that attachment of their vassals which it is so necessary for them to support and preserve. That their fastnesses being laid open, they are deprived of that

security from invasion which they formerly enjoyed. That the bridges, in particular, will render the ordinary people effeminate.

> The middle order say the roads are to them an inconvenience, instead of being useful . . . for their horses being never shod, the gravel would soon whet away their hoofs.

> The lowest class . . . allege that the gravel is intolerable to their naked feet.

In each case the objection is valid, given the traditional expectations of each group.

Forty years later—years which included the second Jacobite rising and the battle of Culloden—Samuel Johnson, probably half a Jacobite in his heart of hearts, writes perceptively but sadly,

> There was perhaps never any change of national manner so quick, so great and so general, as that which has operated in the Highlands, by the last conquest and the subsequent laws . . . The clans retain now little of their original character, their ferocity of temper is softened, their military ardour is extinguished, their dignity of independence is depressed, their contempt of government is subdued, and the reverence for their chiefs abated.

A Lowland Scot, James Boswell, writing in the same year as Johnson, 1773, shall have the last word. He had just met a former member of the Highland Army who described to him the Battle of Culloden. With Culloden, a whole way of life was ended: it was road-building which began this destruction.

> As he narrated the particulars of that ill-advised but brave attempt, I could not refrain from tears. There is a certain association of ideas in my mind upon that subject, by which I am strongly affected. The very Highland names, or the sound of a bag-pipe, will stir my blood, will fill me with a mixture of melancholy and respect for courage; with pity for an unfortunate and superstitious regard for antiquity, and thoughtless inclination for war; in short with a crowd of sensations with which sober rationality has nothing to do.

Book List

There is only one book dealing exclusively with Wade and his roads, that is *Wade in Scotland* by J B Salmond, Moray Press, 1934. It has long been out of print but copies can occasionally be found second-hand.

Dr W Taylor's book, *The Military Roads in Scotland*, David and Charles, 1976, is a fascinating overview of the whole field. Perhaps a third of it deals with Wade.

To continue the story into the mid-nineteenth century, consult *New Ways through the Glens*, Dr A R B Haldane, David and Charles, 1962. This book also deals with the making of the Caledonian Canal.

The eighteenth-century writers from whom we have quoted are;

James Boswell, *Journal of a Tour to The Hebrides*, 1786. There are many modern reprints of this;

E. Burt, *Letters from A Gentleman in the North of Scotland*, 1754. Fifth edition edited by R Jamieson, 1818. There is a facsimile reproduction of this edition published by John Donald, Edinburgh;

Samuel Johnson, *Journey to the Western Isles*, 1775. Again there are many modern reprints;

John Knox, *A Tour Through the Highlands of Scotland in 1786*, 1787. Facsimile reprint by Mercat Press, Edinburgh 1975;

Thomas Newte, *Prospects and Observations on a Tour in England and Scotland*, 1791. This has not been reprinted.

The quotations from Wade's report are taken from Salmond.